LIFE MANAGEMENT SKILLS III

reproducible activity handouts
created for facilitators

A sampler collection of...

aging	nurturance
body image	relapse prevention
communication	relationships
conflict resolution	roles
coping skills	self-awareness
creative expression	self-empowerment
feedback	self-esteem
healthy living	social skills
job readiness	stress management

Kathy L. Korb-Khalsa, OTR/L   Estelle A. Leutenberg   Stacey D. Azok, OTR/L

WELLNESS REPRODUCTIONS & PUBLISHING, LLC
A Guidance Channel Company

We dedicate Life Management Skills III to our children,
who inspire us each and every day of our lives!

Shayna, Arielle and Mason   Kathy, Lynne and Amy   Hannah and Corey

Special thanks to the following therapists, counselors, and educators,
whose submissions of activity handouts for Life Management Skills III were selected.
The Facilitator's Information Sheet on the back of each handout
has a box identifying the submitter(s) and their involvement.

Teresa A. Bachtel, COTA/L

Siri-Dya S. Khalsa, M.Ed.

Deena Baenen, MA, COTA/L

Terri Marshall-Shrader, M.Ed.

Sue Bell-Milby, RNC

Hector L. Merced, OTR/L

Trish Breedlove, OTR/L

Bettie Michelson, MS, OTR

Rebecca Cook, OTR

Christine Miccio, CTRS

Patricia J. Eckwahl, RN

Maggie Moriarty, M.Ed., COTA/L

Dottie D. Gardler, MS, CTRS

Lori Rosenberg, CTRS

Joelean Harl, CTRS

Karen Templeton, RN

Lori Janssen, MSW, LGSW, CADCIII

John R. Way, OTR/L

Pamela A. Joy, COTA/L

Special thanks also to our contributors for "Poetry Power"
who not only shared their poetry, but their hearts:

Jessica Wander *(1st poem)*, Siri-Dya S. Khalsa *(2nd poem)*, and Beth Leslie *(3rd poem)*.

We wish to thank the following family, friends, and associates for their support and feedback.

Frank Azok

Kathleen Kannenberg, MA, OTR

Ken Barker, OTR/L

Jay L. Leutenberg

Eunice Benchell

Jennie Litt

Patricia Clarkson

Gary S. Okin, JD

Susan B. Fine, MA, OTR, FAOTA

The National Association for Poetry Therapy

Serin Foster, National Alliance for the Mentally Ill

National Stigma Clearinghouse

Dr. Frederick J. Frese

Jean Sebastian

Susan Haiman, MPS, OTR/L

Rabbi David C. Seed

Jessica Hargrove

Wellness' Staff

Heights Negative and Plate Staff

Dr. Julie White

Myron Jaffe

David T. Wilkinson

Lynne and David Yulish

FOREWORD

The inspiration for our LIFE MANAGEMENT SKILLS books originated from an ongoing practical need observed within a mental health setting. Handouts had been typically used in treatment as a launching pad for activities, an organizational tool, a visual aid, a tangible reminder of information presented, and as a method for building rapport. However, available handouts often did not meet necessary, high-quality standards in content desired, format, appearance and organization – and lacked permission for reproduction.

We have attempted to meet these standards by offering this sampler collection of handouts which are highly reproducible, organized in a logical manner, designed for specific well-defined purposes, and activity-based, allowing for extensive client involvement. The graphic representations are intentionally different from handout to handout in typestyle, art and design to increase visual appeal, provide variety and clarify meaning.

LIFE MANAGEMENT SKILLS handouts are adaptable and have a broad usage enabling therapists, social workers, nurses, teachers, psychologists, counselors and other professionals to focus on specific goals with their specified populations.

The book has been designed to offer reproducible handouts on the front of each page and nonreproducible facilitator's information on the reverse side. The Facilitator's Information Sheet includes the following sections: Purpose, General Comments and Possible Activities.

We specifically chose spiral binding to allow for easier and accurate reproduction, an especially white paper for clear, sharp copies, and a heavier paper stock for its durability and opacity. If adaptations to any of the handouts are desired, it is recommended to make one copy of the handout, include the changes which will meet *your* specific needs, and then use this copy as the original.

We hope that you will find these handouts in LIFE MANAGEMENT SKILLS III fun, innovative and informative. We wish you much success with your therapeutic and educational endeavors and hope we can continue to be of assistance. Remember . . . creative handouts will hopefully generate creative activities and contribute to a greater sense of WELLNESS!

Wellness Reproductions and Publishing, LLC

Kathy L. Korb-Khalsa *Estelle A. Leutenberg*

THANK YOU TO AMY LEUTENBERG BRODSKY . . .

our Wellness Reproductions and Publishing artist, whose creativity and skill as an illustrator, and experience with clients, continues to give the Life Management Skills books unique, humorous, and meaningful artwork, and whose insights from her clinical work offered guidance on the content as well. Amy Leutenberg Brodsky, LISW, received her Masters of Science in Social Administration from the Mandel School of Applied Social Sciences, Case Western Reserve University. Her art training was received at Kent State University where she achieved a BFA in Studio Art. She continues to pursue her career as an artist, as well as facilitating wellness with children and families in crisis.

WELLNESS REPRODUCTIONS AND PUBLISHING, LLC

is an innovative company which began in 1988. As developers of creative therapeutic and educational products, we have a strong commitment to the mental health profession. Our rapidly growing business began by authoring and self-publishing the book LIFE MANAGEMENT SKILLS I. We have extended our product line to include group presentation posters, therapeutic games, skill building cards, EMOTIONS© identification products, LIFE MANAGEMENT SKILLS II, III, IV, V, VI, SEALS (Self-Esteem and Life Skills) books and corresponding cards, Self-Reflections and Images of Wellness Print series and educational products about serious mental illness. Our books are created with feedback from our customers. Please refer to the last page of this book, our "FEEDBACK" page, and let us hear from YOU!

A Guidance Channel Company

P.O. Box 760 • Plainview, New York 11803-0760
800 / 669-9208 • FAX: 800 / 501-8120
e-mail: info@wellness-resources.com • website: http://wellness-resources.com

TABLE OF CONTENTS

Page numbers are on the Facilitator's Information Sheet, located on the reverse side of each handout.

♀ *symbol denotes pages with a women's focus,*
♂ *symbol denotes pages with a men's focus.*

* *presentation poster available (see order form - last page)*   [over for Supplemental Section]

TABLE OF CONTENTS

It's never too early... or late... to take 21 STEPS to...
AGING SUCCESSFULLY!

Complete the following self-assessment by marking the number in each step, on a scale from 1 to 5 (1, "not-at-all" to 5, "all-the-time").

Review each *step* along the way to evaluate how well you are taking care of yourself!

ARE YOU...

- making time for solitude?
- touching nature each week?
- listening to your inner-voice?
- getting quality rest and sleep?
- actively managing your stress?
- finding support, and giving it back?
- releasing uncomfortable emotions?
- giving and receiving affection? hugs?
- getting daily or weekly spiritual nourishment?
- forgiving yourself when you make a mistake?
- doing things that give you a sense of fulfillment, joy and purpose?
- "cutting your losses" and moving on with your life after a tragedy or setback?
- taking care of your skin by decreasing sun exposure, using a sunscreen and a good lotion?
- challenging yourself to develop or learn new skills, languages, hobbies, sports, interests, and/or activities?
- exercising (with physician's approval) by stretching and regular aerobic exercise, e.g., walking, swimming, or working out?
- surrounding yourself with optimistic friends, associates, and relatives who possess a healthy sense of humor? nurturing friendships?
- keeping an active, but varied and balanced schedule which includes leisure time (time for yourself, time to play, time to treat or reward yourself)?
- sharing yourself by contributing to society, involving yourself in at least one meaningful cause, e.g., government, church/synagogue, community, special projects, etc.?
- continually evaluating your physical appearance, and changing, when it's appropriate, to meet your specific age's needs, e.g., hair length and styles, clothing length and styles, shoes, etc.?
- scheduling and keeping regular appointments for physical, visual, dental, emotional and all other needs? monitoring your men's/women's health needs? following doctor's recommendations?
- working on your health by: not smoking; maintaining good nutrition, a healthy weight, and eating something fresh and unprocessed every day; getting adequate calcium, fiber, and water; controlling alcohol, cholesterol and caffeine intake?

Write a list of GOALS at least every 3 months to keep a clear, focused direction!

Add up your score		
	21-41	Change your ways — you can do it!
	42-62	Just so-so — keep working at it!
	63-83	Good work — challenge yourself even more!
	84-105	You're aging successfully — bravo! Keep it up!

Total score:

AGING SUCCESSFULLY!

I. PURPOSE:

To promote successful aging by increasing awareness of 21 components to healthy aging.

II. GENERAL COMMENTS:

Successful aging begins with an attitude of taking a wholistic view of oneself. By addressing physical, emotional, social, spiritual, and intellectual aspects, one can make realistic goals for the future.

III. POSSIBLE ACTIVITIES:

A. 1. Open discussion of obstacles to healthy aging, e.g.,

    a. common phrases: "old timer"; "aging parent"; "over-the-hill"; "senior citizen"; "drives like an old lady"; etc.

    b. media: make-up advertisement; youthful models; "plight of the elderly" on the news; too few older characters on TV commercials, and they are usually advertising dentures, tonics, laxatives, arthritis medication, etc. Today's TV shows tend to not feature older stars, as compared to shows in the past like "Green Acres", "Beverly Hillbillies", "Gomer Pyle", "Waltons", etc.

    c. common images: retire automatically at age 65 or younger; helpless; senile; dependent; solitary; poor old people; sick; lonely; retired; childish; decrepit; lost their teeth; forgetful; dozing in a rocking chair; repeat themselves; walk slowly; dislike changes; set in their ways; talk about "the good old days"; etc.

2. Present handout as a pro-active approach to healthy aging.

3. Ask each group member to read aloud a step, and explain it's importance, and then follow the self-assessment scale provided on the front of the handout.

4. Instruct group members to total their score and to set goals after reviewing 1 or 2 of the lower scores.

5. Discuss and support goals.

6. Process benefits of a healthy approach to aging.

B. 1. Discuss concept of healthy aging. Distribute handouts and instruct group members to complete.

2. Share totals and determine action plans, with group input as needed.

3. Distribute a variety of magazines to group, including several geared to the older adult population.

4. Instruct group members to work together to construct a group collage focusing on healthy aging. Encourage them to cut-out pictures/words/phrases that elicit positive aging images, e.g., older adults exercising, working, cooking healthy foods, socializing, etc.

5. Encourage group to give a title to the collage which best represents their views of healthy aging.

6. Display complete collage in a conspicuous place for greater awareness of healthy aging.

7. Process benefits of this activity.

STAY YOUNG AT HEART!

HOW COULD YOU...

♥ FEEL MORE PRODUCTIVE? _____

♡ MAKE A FRIEND? _____

♥ LEARN SOMETHING NEW? _____

♡ HELP SOMEONE? _____

♥ PLAN SOMETHING SPECIAL? _____

♡ DO SOMETHING THOUGHTFUL? _____

♥ ADD ENJOYMENT TO EACH DAY? _____

♡ EXPAND YOUR INTERESTS? _____

♥ BE MORE FLEXIBLE? _____

♡ MAKE CONSTRUCTIVE CHANGES? _____

♥ SHOW YOUR LOVE? _____

♡ _____

I. PURPOSE:

To help develop a positive approach to life as people age.

II. GENERAL COMMENTS:

Changes in lifestyle, friends, self-image, pleasures and health may occur in later life.
Measurable and realistic goals empower an individual and offer a positive outlook for the future.

III. POSSIBLE ACTIVITIES:

A. 1. Encourage group members to answer as many questions as would be appropriate for them.

2. Facilitate a discussion by asking members to share their answers and promote the brainstorming of ideas.

3. Make available information of local and regional services, facilities, events, and organizations for seniors, along with programs such as Elderhostel: 75 Federal Street
Boston, MA 02110-1941
(617) 426-7788

and the services of
the American Association of Retired Persons (AARP): 601 E Street NW
Washington, DC 20049
(202) 434-2277

4. Encourage each member to prioritize these goals and make more detailed plans for one or more.

5. Process benefits of this activity.

B. 1. Develop a card game from the handout by cutting paper into strips – one question per strip.

2. Place strips in basket. Ask group members to choose a strip and answer it personally and honestly.

3. Distribute handouts and instruct group members to choose only three that they need to work on.

4. Instruct them to write goals on the provided line adjacent to their chosen three, e.g., Add enjoyment to each day: I will appreciate nature by spending outdoor time at least five minutes each day.

5. Make sure goals are realistic and measurable.

6. Process by sharing goals and offering feedback and support.

Activity handout and facilitator's information submitted by Bettie Michelson, MS, OTR, De Kalb, IL.

BODY IMAGE JOURNAL

Certain events in our lives can trigger negative thoughts / negative self-talk in regard to our bodies, which can then trigger negative feelings and actions. This vicious cycle is self-defeating and damaging to our self-image and our sense of well-being. First, write in an event which affects your body image. Identify your negative self-talk, related feelings, and resulting actions. Then, as a reframing exercise, list positive self-talk statements you can say to influence your feelings and actions in a healthy way.

EVENT	(–) SELF-TALK	FEELINGS	ACTIONS	(+) SELF-TALK	FEELINGS	ACTIONS
Going shopping and trying on clothes for a special occasion.	*"I'm so fat!"* *"How could I have gained all this weight back?"* *"I'm so stupid and lazy."*	*disgust* *anger* *guilt* *embarrassment* *regret*	• *abruptly leave the store in tears.* • *swear I'll never shop or buy clothes again.* • *eat junk food on the way home.*	*"I'll need to wear a larger size for now."* *"I'll begin eating healthier & exercising by next week."* *"I've been able to lose weight before and I will do it again."*	*confidence* *pride* *determination* *hope* *satisfaction*	• *Purchase an outfit that is comfortable and flattering at my present weight.* • *Begin a healthy exercise and eating plan.* • *Communicate feelings to others.*

BODY IMAGE JOURNAL

I. PURPOSE:

To develop body-image awareness.

To increase self-esteem by observing, recording, and evaluating key events related to body image.

II. GENERAL COMMENTS:

Body image, the way one views one's own body, is a sensitive and important topic. Self-talk related to body image directly affects one's feelings and actions in a particular situation. Being able to identify negative self-talk first, and then to reframe that self-talk, is a skill that can significantly improve one's overall self-image. Journals can assist in the awareness and skill development process by allowing one to (1) recall events related to body image, (2) record them in a logical, organized way, (3) evaluate them, and (4) identify alternate responses. When recalling events, it's important to consider the entire scope of one's body image, including weight, skin / complexion, hair, body type and features, posture, capabilities, etc.

III. POSSIBLE ACTIVITIES:

This handout may be used in conjunction with MIRROR MIRROR... (page 4).

A. 1. Discuss definition of body image and individual's own experiences with this area. Elaborate on information provided in General Comments above.

2. Brainstorm on chalkboard a list of events that may potentially affect one's body image.

3. Choose one event generated by group or use example below to illustrate concept of body image journal.

4. Distribute handouts to all group members and discuss additional example on front.

5. Instruct group members to identify 2 or 3 of their own events and complete the handout appropriately.

6. When members have finished their handouts, reconvene and discuss as a group.

7. Encourage all group members to continue journaling on own as an ongoing self-development exercise.

8. Process benefits of this activity.

B. 1. Facilitate discussion of women's body image vs. men's body image – how are each affected by changing times? the media? our peers?

2. Teach group the assertive right of both sexes "...take pride in my body and define attractiveness in my own terms." See Life Management Skills II, Assertive Rights, Page 9!

3. Distribute handouts to all group members and discuss additional example on front.

4. Instruct group members to identify 2 or 3 of their own events and complete the handout appropriately.

5. Share as a group the variety of responses.

6. Process this activity by reminding group of factors that influence body image, their assertive right as stated in B.2. and the potential benefits of using a journal.

Mirror, Mirror on the Wall...

What's my BODY IMAGE after all?

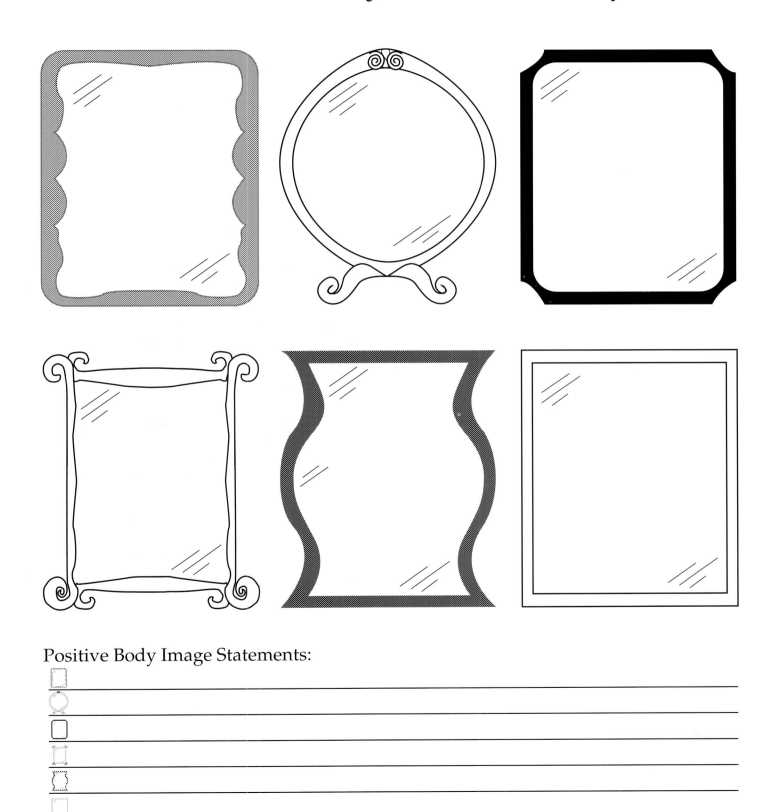

Positive Body Image Statements:

_____

_____

_____

_____

_____

_____

Mirror, Mirror on the Wall...

I. PURPOSE:

To develop body image awareness.

To increase awareness of what may influence body image.

To create body image affirmations.

II. GENERAL COMMENTS:

Body image, the way one views one's own body, is a sensitive and important topic for women in particular. Society sends many powerful messages to women regarding the "appropriate" and/or "desirable" body. Consider that in the 1970's, department store mannequins were typically size 10-12, today those mannequins are size 3-5. Consider also the rising number of women with various eating disorders as the pressure to be "thin" increases. Identifying and defining a realistic, personal body image is an important step for women in developing healthy self-acceptance and esteem.

III. POSSIBLE ACTIVITIES:

A. 1. Encourage group members to list in each box, on the first row, an aspect of their body and/or appearance that they like.

2. Instruct group members to write in each of the three boxes, on the second row, characteristics of a "good" body as affirmed by society or others in their life.

3. Discuss the members' responses...

a. Which row was easier to fill in and why?
b. What are the messages that society sends to women about their bodies?

4. Assist group members in writing several affirmative statements about their bodies.

5. Process the importance of affirming one's body and separating one's personal image from that created by society and/or others.

6. Suggest group members follow up this activity at home by privately looking at their naked bodies in a mirror and affirming aloud three things they like about what they see.

B. 1. Instruct group members to write their name in the first box on their handout.

2. Tell members to fill in each remaining box with a group member's name until the name of each group member is written in a separate box (photocopy additional handouts if necessary).

3. Ask members to write one positive statement in the box with their name on it.

4. Continue by writing one positive statement about the body of the person's name in each box.

5. Cut or tear the boxes and have the members deliver them to each other or post them on pieces of butcher paper with each group member's name on them.

6. Encourage members to quietly read the statements they receive.

7. Discuss the following:

a. Do you feel the statements you received are true? Why or why not?
b. Which, if any, of the statements surprised you?
c. Which ones are the easiest to believe? The most difficult to believe? Why?
d. What conclusions had you drawn about your body prior to this exercise? What were these conclusions based on?
e. Was it difficult to write positive statements for others? Why?
f. Were you using your own norms, the norms of significant others and/or the norms of society in what you looked for as "positive" in others' bodies?

8. Assist group members in writing several affirmative statements about their bodies.

9. Process the importance of using positive feedback, affirming one's body, and distinguishing one's personal body image from that created by society and/or others.

10. Suggest group members follow up this activity at home by privately looking at their naked bodies in a mirror and affirming aloud three things they like about what they see.

Activity handout and facilitator's information submitted by Terri Marshall-Schrader, M. Ed., San Antonio, TX.

BROKEN RECORD technique

The *broken-record* is an assertive technique which attempts to get your point across. It is recommended to repeat your message clearly and emphatically, over and over and over again, without changing your wording . . . to make sure that you are heard!!

Situations in which the *broken-record* technique might be helpful. . .

1. _____

2. _____

3. _____

It would be helpful to me to use the *broken-record* technique with . . .

_____
_____.

This technique would be beneficial to my communication with others because . . .

_____
_____.

After using this technique, I will probably feel . . .

_____
_____.

BROKEN
RECORD
technique

I. PURPOSE:

To gain understanding of the assertive *broken-record* technique.

To increase communication skills by practicing the *broken-record* technique.

II. GENERAL COMMENTS:

The assertive technique referred to as the *broken-record* is especially helpful when responding to or confronting manipulative and/or aggressive behavior. It involves repeating a message several times, with no deviation, in an attempt to get a point across and be heard. The person on the receiving end usually responds in the way desired, often to get the repetitive message to stop. As with other assertive techniques, it requires a clear, direct, honest, and specific approach.

III. POSSIBLE ACTIVITIES:

A. 1. Distribute handouts to all group members.

2. Discuss the *broken-record* technique as described on front of handout. Include discussion of group members' experiences with this technique.

3. Ask members to identify three situations in which they could use practice with this technique.

4. Instruct group members to read their situations aloud.

5. Taking turns, encourage group members to choose one of their three situations that they would like to see role-played. Continue with each member initiating one role-play.

6. Encourage support and feedback from others.

7. Process benefits of using this assertive technique by completing three questions on handout and discussing.

B. 1. Explain the *broken-record* technique.

2. Distribute handouts.

3. List roles that group members are presently involved in, e.g., spouse, friend, employee, etc.

4. Discuss the specific roles in which this technique might be the most useful to group members.

5. Ask individuals to identify a specific situation where this technique might be useful.

6. Instruct individuals to role-play those that require practice!

7. Complete bottom of handout.

8. Process benefits of using this assertive technique.

Passive – AGGRESSIVE

Passive -**AGGRESSIVE** is a category of behavior and communication associated with indirect aggression. It takes the form of a passive, but non-confrontive style.

Meet
PATRICIA
Passive-**AGGRESSIVE**

Meet
PATRICK
Passive-**AGGRESSIVE**

Hi! I'm sarcastic and sly – often feeling one way, but doing something else. I like to be critical of advice and direction of others. Sulking, pouting, dawdling, procrastinating and being chronically late are common characteristics of my behavior. Negative and pessimistic, I often feel like a victim and have difficulty accepting responsibility. Sometimes, I dress inappropriately for social or occupational activities. At work, I sabotage the efforts of others and often have educational and social failures. I often feel envious and resentful and am subtly antagonistic.

Helpful strategies in dealing with *Passive* -AGGRESSIVE traits . . .

- encourage ventilation and space for anger
- offer consistency and rules
- model assertive responses
- try humor and openness
- confront behavior directly
- _____

Passive -AGGRESSIVE

I. PURPOSE:

To increase communication by recognizing passive-aggressive traits and helpful strategies to deal with them.

To increase communication by practicing assertive responses.

II. GENERAL COMMENTS:

In an assertiveness model, this is the fourth category of communication or behavior. Indirect aggression leads to resentful, unhealthy relationships. In contrast, assertion is the method of communication recommended. It will enhance the integrity and self-esteem of both parties and will lead to more fulfilling relationships.

III. POSSIBLE ACTIVITIES:

A. 1. Distribute handouts and read aloud as a group.

2. Divide the group into dyads, asking each pair to write a brief (1-2 pp.) skit from their own observed experiences, e.g., within their spousal interactions, a work-related scenario, customer/salesperson verbal exchange, etc.

3. Ask each dyad to role-play the skit, first in the original passive-aggressive style and then in the more assertive style, utilizing the helpful strategy suggestion.

4. Encourage active listening of group members by asking that they provide feedback to role-players.

5. Process by asking group members to identify passive-aggressive traits discussed, without looking at their handouts, and helpful strategies they can use to increase assertiveness.

B. 1. Distribute handouts and read aloud as a group.

2. Brainstorm on chalkboard a list of situations that represent passive-aggressive behavior.

3. Write each one identified on a separate piece of paper and place in a basket.

4. Randomly ask a group member to choose a paper from the basket and choose one other group member to do a role-play with him/her, focused on the chosen situation.

5. Support assertive responses.

6. Continue until all group members have role-played.

7. Process benefits of activity.

We Are People With ...

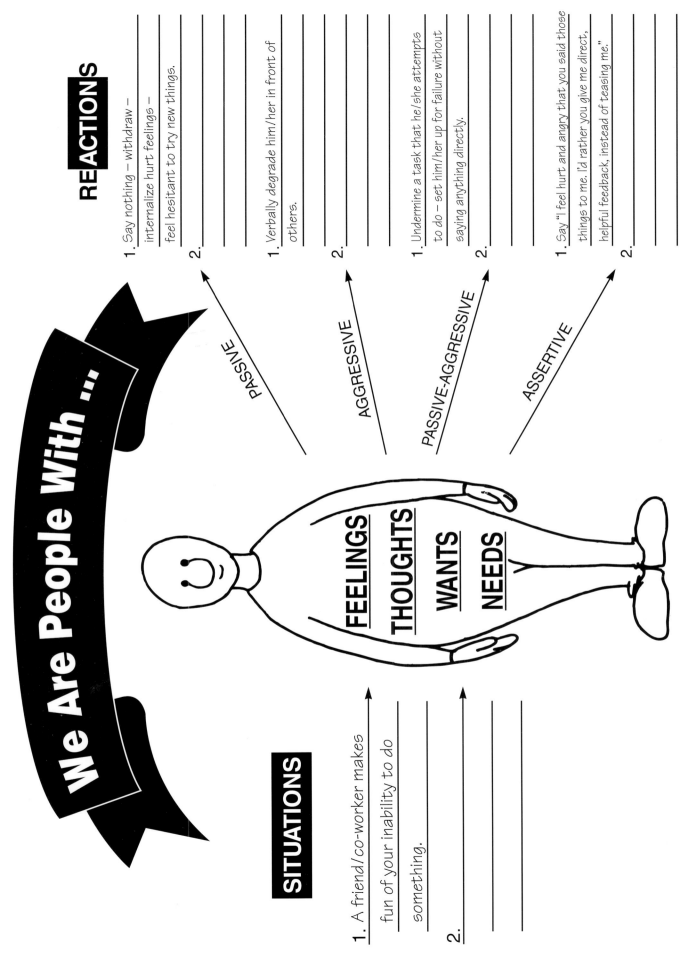

REACTIONS

PASSIVE

1. Say nothing – withdraw – internalize hurt feelings – feel hesitant to try new things.

2.

AGGRESSIVE

1. Verbally degrade him/her in front of others.

2.

PASSIVE-AGGRESSIVE

1. Undermine a task that he/she attempts to do – set him/her up for failure without saying anything directly.

2.

ASSERTIVE

1. Say "I feel hurt and angry that you said those things to me. I'd rather you give me direct, helpful feedback, instead of teasing me."

2.

FEELINGS
THOUGHTS
WANTS
NEEDS

SITUATIONS

1. A friend/co-worker makes fun of your inability to do something.

2.

We Are People With ...

I. PURPOSE:

To promote assertiveness by increasing awareness of our choices of communication styles.

II. GENERAL COMMENTS:

Awareness of choices in communication is the first step to assertion. The "we are people" exercise visually ties in the relationship between situations and reactions to increase this awareness.

III. POSSIBLE ACTIVITIES:

A. 1. Present the handout to individuals.

  2. Explain and define the 4 communication styles or reactions:

  PASSIVE - I do not have a right to my feelings, thoughts, wants and needs, but others do have that right. So . . .
  Example - I am quiet.
  I don't make decisions.
  I go along with others.

  AGGRESSIVE - I have a right to my feelings, thoughts, wants and needs, but others have no rights. So . . .
  Example - I am loud.
  I am always right.
  I demand my way.

  PASSIVE - AGGRESSIVE - I have no rights and others don't either. So . . .
  Example - I refuse to communicate.
  I seek revenge in sneaky ways (hidden agenda).
  I don't listen and I don't talk.
  I am sarcastic.

  ASSERTIVE - I have a right to my feelings, thoughts, wants and needs, and others have a right to their feelings, thoughts, wants, and needs. So . . .
  Example - I state how I feel and I listen to how you feel.
  I make decisions, but I'm also willing to compromise.
  I'm honest, direct and speak openly.

  3. Instruct individuals to complete the handout by using the following examples of situations:

  Personal -   fears - e.g., war
                    failures - e.g., loss of job
                    health conditions - e.g., limited handicapped access

  Social -   parents / spouse - e.g., divorce
                    death / loss
                    activities - e.g., closure of bowling alley

  Environmental -   alcohol / drugs
                    job / school pressures
                    moving

  4. Process benefits of this activity and discuss action plans.

B. 1. Instruct group members to break into groups of 5 and present each group with a handout.

  2. Ask group members to brainstorm possible situations that they may or may not have control over and choose 3 to write on the handout.

  3. Under Reactions, again encourage members to brainstorm reactions for each of the 4 communication styles.

  4. Reconvene as a large group and share responses.

  5. Role-play situations, identifying reactions.

Activity handout and facilitator's information submitted by Rebecca Cook, OTR, Petersburg, MI.

RESOLVING CONFLICTS

CONFLICT ⟺ RESOLUTION

Describe:
A. The Situation
B. What You'd Like to Change

Describe:
A. Your Role/Responsibility in Making the Change
B. The Other's Role/Responsibility in Making the Change

1 A: _____

_____

_____

B: _____

_____

_____

1 A: My Role/Responsibility: _____

_____

_____

B: _____ Role/Responsibility:

_____

_____

2 A: _____

_____

_____

B: _____

_____

_____

2 A: My Role/Responsibility:_____

_____

_____

B: _____ Role/Responsibility:

_____

_____

3 A: _____

_____

_____

B: _____

_____

_____

3 A: My Role/Responsibility:_____

_____

_____

B: _____ Role/Responsibility:

_____

_____

Resolving Conflicts

I. PURPOSE:

To increase conflict resolution skills.

To increase ability to own responsibility for one's behavior in a particular conflict situation.

II. GENERAL COMMENTS:

Conflict arises between people in a wide variety of situations. When the individuals lack specific conflict resolution skills, communication breaks down and blaming/not owning responsibility for behaviors can occur. It can be nearly impossible to resolve a conflict if either or both individuals do not accept responsibility for their own roles in the situation. On the positive side, however, change and conflict resolution can take place when roles are clearly identified and agreed upon between the individuals involved.

III. POSSIBLE ACTIVITIES:

A. 1. Distribute handouts and discuss purpose of activity, focusing on information in GENERAL COMMENTS section.

2. Ask group members to rate themselves on a scale of 1-10 (1–lowest, 10–highest) in regards to conflict resolution skills/ability.

3. Allow 15-20 minutes for group members to complete handout after first discussing the following example:

CONFLICT	RESOLUTION
1a. My mother-in-law and I don't agree on child-rearing techniques.	1a. My role/responsibility: I need to clearly identify the rules for the children and assert myself with her re: following through with them.
b. I'd like her to adhere to my rules for my children when she babysits.	b. Mother-in-law's role/responsibility: Listen to my concerns, express her differences, and offer compromises if needed.

4. When all group members have completed handouts, discuss as a group, at least one of each group member's conflict situations and potential resolutions.

5. Facilitate feedback and support from others.

6. Encourage group members to share proposed resolutions with the involved individuals, as able.

7. Process the benefits of developing conflict resolution skills.

B. 1. Distribute handouts and discuss purpose of activity, focusing on information in GENERAL COMMENTS section.

2. Ask group members for an example, and illustrate process on chalkboard.

3. Use these "potential" situations to further demonstrate resolutions.

Conflict A: My boss screams at me in front of my colleagues.

B: I'd like him/her to stop/talk to me in private.

Conflict A: My friend is always late in picking me up.

B: I'd like him/her to call if she's late/stop being so late.

4. Give group members 10 minutes to complete handout.

5. Discuss as a group each person's conflicts and resolutions and role-play, as able, process of discussing roles and responsibilities with the other person. Support assertive communication skills.

6. Process the benefits of developing conflict resolution skills.

Activity handout submitted by and facilitator's information adapted from submission by Trish Breedlove, OTR/L, Canton, OH.

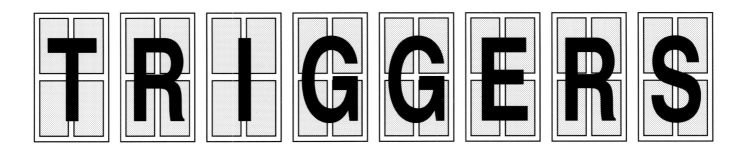

TRIGGERS

*"Triggers" – set us off to destructive behavior. They can be **internal** (self-thoughts or emotions) or **external** (situations, events, or what people say or do).*

They usually elicit feelings of fear or anger. Oftentimes, to get rid of these uncomfortable and overwhelming feelings, people drink alcohol, use street and/or prescription drugs, eat, etc., or a combination of destructive behaviors, to eliminate the "pain".

The emotional "pain" is not actually eliminated --- it still remains.

*Our "triggers" need to be looked at carefully. They serve as **WINDOWS** to our inner-selves.*

MONITOR YOURSELF FOR A DAY:

DAY: _____

DESCRIBE THE SITUATION: _____

_____

_____

EXTERNAL TRIGGERS:		INTERNAL TRIGGERS:	
1	2	1	2
3	4	3	4

BEHAVIOR: _____

_____

_____

Was I satisfied with my behavior?　☐ Yes　　☐ No

What could I do differently in the future? _____

_____

_____

TRIGGERS

I. PURPOSE:

To increase self-awareness of internal and external "triggers", and the feelings and behaviors they elicit.

II. GENERAL COMMENTS:

The concept of "triggers" is often used by the twelve-step model, but can be generalized to non-recovery issues as well. Destructive behavior can include, not only alcohol or drug use, but also inappropriate risk taking, or even self-abusive acts. "Triggers" can happen quickly, and the response is often like a "knee-jerk" reaction, yielding undesirable consequences. Self-monitoring the entire course of events assists in evaluating the process.

III. POSSIBLE ACTIVITIES:

A. 1. Illustrate the concept of "triggers" by using the analogy "What lights our fuse?". List on the chalkboard both internal and external triggers as defined on the front of the handout.

2. Discuss as a group which is more powerful for them – internal or external, facilitating insights wherever possible.

3. Distribute handouts and instruct group members to complete, using today or yesterday for the self-monitoring activity.

4. Choose 1-2 individuals to share their situation, triggers, and behaviors, encouraging group interaction.

5. Complete the exercise by reviewing the bottom box and again asking for group feedback.

6. Process the group by reviewing the internal and external triggers, and asking group members to outline the steps of self-monitoring without looking at their handouts. Offer the handout to all as a homework assignment.

B. 1. Discuss the concept of "triggers", differentiating between external and internal triggers as described on front of handout.

2. Encourage group members to write on strips of paper 1 external trigger and 1 internal trigger.

3. Mix all members' strips of paper together in a basket and pass around, asking each member to choose 2 strips.

4. Instruct group members to take turns and read the 2 triggers they chose from the basket, first identifying them as internal or external and then, how they might respond to them.

5. Encourage group feedback and ask the persons who originally wrote the triggers, to identify themselves and their usual or typical responses.

6. Distribute handouts, and ask members to complete for next session.

7. Process benefits of this activity.

Activity handout and facilitator's information adapted from TRIGGERS OF ANGER by Trish Breedlove, OTR/L, Canton, OH.

DO YOU FEEL LIKE YOU'RE IN THE
MIDDLE OF A SANDWICH?

Children Grandchildren					Fill in the initials of your family members in the top boxes. Then, mark the boxes with a Y = yes, N = no, or / = not applicable, to evaluate your situation and feelings.	Parents Grandparents				
					Am I dissatisfied with the amount of time I spend with them? (either too much or too little)					
					Is the level of involvement in each other's lives unhealthy for me?					
					Do I have difficulty allowing them to be as independent as they can possibly be?					
					Do I get stress symptoms when I'm with them? (need to eat, drink, have stomach problems, headaches, etc.)					
					Do I have difficulty expressing my feelings and needs to them in an open, honest and direct way?					
					Do I resent the responsibilities that I have? (financial, transportation, housekeeping, shopping, laundry, etc.)					
					Does this person try to give *guilt trips* (verbally or nonverbally) when I take time for myself?					
					Do I resent my dependence on them for financial, emotional, lifestyle needs?					
					Do I feel pressured by others regarding the way I give support/care?					
					Do I feel trapped?					

It is important to be aware of a variety of emotions... YOU ARE NOT ALONE!

DO YOU FEEL...

hopeful	angry	sad	anxious	frustrated	guilty	annoyed	confused	satisfied	discouraged	helpless	regretful

Hints for Caregivers

- Let someone you trust take over for a while, so you can take a long walk, exercise, get a good night's sleep, etc.
- Contact a local mental health center.
- Go browse at a bookstore – buy a joke book!
- Try a sad movie (if you can't cry, but need to).
- Call a support group – or organize one! Blow off steam and share!
- Organize yourself – put articles, brochures, medical forms and other pertinent information in a notebook.
- Create an environment that meets your needs (music, reading material, fresh air, etc.) during caregiving times.
- Incorporate your own errands when doing errands for others: haircut, grocery, pharmacy, doctor, dentist, shopping, laundry, etc.
- Visit your local recreation center or gym to check activities offered. Try to get other family members to assist.

Read This List Everyday:
You Have The Right To...

Take Care of Yourself

Seek Help From Others

Express Uncomfortable Feelings to Others

Reject Relative's Attempt to Manipulate

Request Consideration from Relative

Judge Your Own Decisions and Behavior and Feel Comfortable with the Way You're Handling the Situation

Protect Your Individuality

Make a Life for Yourself

Change the Situation, Exploring Options and Respecting Your Choices

MIDDLE OF A SANDWICH?

I. PURPOSE:

To increase awareness of the obligations and demands of being in the "sandwich generation".

To increase role satisfaction within this complex situation.

II. GENERAL COMMENTS:

The "sandwich generation" refers to those who find themselves responsible for both their parents' and children's welfare. With the amount of people over age 65 increasing, more adults are having to cope with their aging parents moving in while they are still raising their own children. Oftentimes, it is the females in the family who have this responsibility, but not necessarily. Juggling the caregiving responsibilities as well as other roles such as: worker, student, friend, etc., can easily be overwhelming and stressful. Although care of a spouse may not technically be associated with the "sandwich generation" concept, if caregiving becomes a responsibility, this may also create a great deal of stress for an individual. Consideration needs to be given to all areas of stress identified with caregiving.

III. POSSIBLE ACTIVITIES:

A. 1. Write the word "caregiver" on the chalkboard.

2. Ask group members to list everyone/everything (people, pets, plants) they *give care to.*

3. Elicit "emotions" group members have as they look at that list.

4. Distribute handouts and ask group members to complete, discussing emotions, hints for caregivers and the "rights" list.

5. Process by reviewing with group members the meaning of "sandwich generation", "hints", and "rights".

B. 1. Discuss "sandwich generation" concept, and briefly, how members have experienced it in their lives.

2. Distribute handouts to all group members and allow 5-10 minutes to complete.

3. Pair group members for discussion of their responses and instruct them to identify one "hint" and one "right" that they will begin incorporating into their daily lives immediately.

4. Reconvene as a large group and share a summary of each pair's responses.

5. Encourage all group members to keep the lower half of the handout in a conspicuous place (refrigerator, purse/wallet, bulletin board, etc.) to remind them of caregivers' "hints" and "rights".

6. Process the benefits of this activity.

POSITIVE FOCUS

Picture these images to
help you focus on a
POSITIVE MENTAL ATTITUDE!

Picture a time or situation when
you felt proud of yourself.

Picture one positive
thing you do well.

Picture one of your roles
or responsibilities in which
you feel positive.

Picture one positive way you stay
healthy or take care of your body.

Picture one positive characteristic
you like best about yourself.

Picture one positive way you
communicate or relate to others.

Picture one positive way
you stay young at heart.

Picture one positive way
you cope with stress.

Picture one way you can help
yourself stay positive.

Positive **Focus**

I. PURPOSE:

To increase coping skills by developing a positive focus.

II. GENERAL COMMENTS:

A positive mental focus helps insulate us from negativity. When we focus on positives regarding our personality, activities, image, etc., we reflect this positive persona onto ourselves and others.

III. POSSIBLE ACTIVITIES:

A. 1. Discuss the benefits of a positive focus and how it correlates with self-esteem.

2. Encourage individuals to complete the handout.

3. Ask group members to share their three favorite ones.

4. Process the benefits of this activity with the group.

B. 1. Discuss the benefits of a positive focus and how it correlates with self-esteem.

2. Encourage individuals to complete the handout and put their names at the top of the page.

3. Collect all handouts and redistribute, making sure group members do not get their own papers.

4. Ask each group member to take turns reading aloud the papers they were given, without identifying whose paper it is.

5. Encourage the others to guess the author of each paper; when s/he is correctly identified, ask her/him to state how it felt to complete the handout and have it shared with others.

6. Continue until all group members have shared.

7. Process benefits of a positive focus.

Activity handout and facilitator's information adapted from submission by Pamela A. Joy, COTA/L, N. Canton, OH.

Positive Mental Attitude

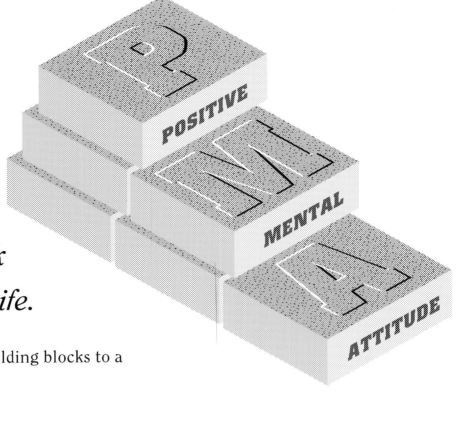

*is an upbeat,
optimistic outlook
or perception on life.*

Take a look at these three building blocks to a
Positive Mental Attitude.

P is for POSITIVE

I remain *positive* by having plans for my future. They are:

1. _____
2. _____
3. _____

M is for MENTAL

Mental statements that will help me meet my above plans are:

1. _____
2. _____
3. _____

A is for ATTITUDE

My *attitude* can be influenced by acknowledging the assets I possess, or have in my environment, to help me meet
my above plans. My assets are:

1. _____
2. _____
3. _____

Positive Mental Attitude

I. PURPOSE:

To increase coping skills by becoming aware of three components of a *positive mental attitude*.

II. GENERAL COMMENTS:

Positive mental attitude is an upbeat, optimistic outlook or perception on life. A *positive mental attitude* can be achieved when we identify our internal and external strengths when dealing with stress or working towards a goal.

III. POSSIBLE ACTIVITIES:

A. 1. Discuss with group members the definition of *positive mental attitude* as stated on front of handout.

   2. Complete as a group, reviewing and explaining each section at a time, using the following example:

     P – "I want to learn how to play the piano."

     M – "It is difficult to try something new, but I *know* I can do it."

     A – "I'm a quick learner."

   3. Encourage feedback and support among group members.

   4. Process benefits of this activity.

B. 1. Discuss with group members the definition of *positive mental attitude* as stated on front of handout.

   2. Complete as a group, reviewing and explaining each section at a time, using the following example:

     P – "I want to learn how to play the piano."

     M – "It is difficult to try something new, but I *know* I can do it."

     A – "I'm a quick learner."

   3. Instruct group members to choose one plan to complete while they are in your facility.

   4. Keep track of efforts made to complete the chosen plan. Give verbal or physical positive reinforcements.

   5. Give a reward for completion of plan, possibly a certificate of achievement.

   6. Process benefits of this activity.

Activity handout and facilitator's information adapted from submission by Pamela A. Joy, COTA/L, N. Canton, OH.

SEEKING
Solitude

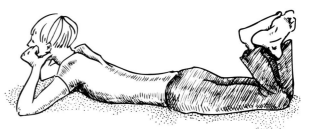

Spending time by ourselves each day, without feeling a sense of loneliness, is essential to our overall well-being. Solitude offers us a chance to self-reflect, and to replenish ourselves when we are overwhelmed by the responsibilities we have in our day-to-day lives. Enjoying solitude often does not come naturally for individuals . . . it is a life skill that needs to be learned and then nurtured. Many individuals spend time by themselves, but perceive this "alone-ness" primarily as "loneliness".

Listed below are two ways in which we might perceive ALONE TIME. Try reading these descriptions to see if you have been experiencing either or both of these recently. Then, using symbols or pictures, draw an image of each experience.

(my image)

LONELINESS
- ❑ solitaire
- ❑ without companions
- ❑ sad
- ❑ not often visited
- ❑ remote
- ❑ distant
- ❑ isolated
- ❑ separated
- ❑ unsupported
- ❑ closed off
- ❑ _____
- ❑ _____

SOLITUDE
- ❑ serene
- ❑ calm
- ❑ content
- ❑ reflective
- ❑ quiet
- ❑ not with others
- ❑ relaxed
- ❑ peaceful
- ❑ spirit-ful
- ❑ nurtured
- ❑ _____
- ❑ _____

(my image)

TRUE SOLITUDE REQUIRES US TO BE COMFORTABLE WITH BEING ALONE –
TO ENJOY THE "ME" INSIDE <u>EACH</u> OF US, DAY AFTER DAY AFTER DAY . . .

SEEKING
Solitude

I. PURPOSE:

To increase coping skills by evaluating how ALONE TIME is perceived . . . as loneliness or as solitude.

To increase use of solitude as a coping skill.

II. GENERAL COMMENTS:

Time spent alone can be perceived as loneliness or as solitude, and can significantly affect one's sense of well-being. Experiencing alone time as loneliness, especially over a long period of time or on a frequent basis, contributes to emotional distress and needs to be addressed – either by changing one's perception or by changing one's lifestyle to reflect less alone time. Solitude is a healthy experience of alone time which can be used as an effective coping skill on a daily basis.

III. POSSIBLE ACTIVITIES:

A. 1. Distribute handouts and read aloud.

2. Encourage group members to discuss fully the difference between feelings of loneliness and feelings of solitude. Provide thought-provoking questions, such as: Can you spend time alone without feeling lonely? What are some pleasant memories you have of solitude? Have you ever experienced loneliness when with others? etc.

3. Ask group members to complete handouts, first checking off those characteristics of loneliness and solitude frequently experienced (in last 2-3 weeks), and then drawing an image that represents each of these experiences.

4. Discuss, as a group, all responses and facilitate feedback from members.

5. Emphasize use of solitude on a daily basis as a healthy coping skill.

6. Process benefits of decreasing loneliness time and increasing solitude time.

B. 1. Introduce topic of solitude as a coping skill.

2. Brainstorm as many words as possible associated with loneliness and solitude. List on chalkboard.

3. Distribute handouts and read aloud.

4. Encourage group members to discuss fully the difference between feelings of loneliness and feelings of solitude. Provide thought-provoking questions, such as: Can you spend time alone without feeling lonely? What are some pleasant memories you have of solitude? Have you ever experienced loneliness when with others? etc.

5. Divide large group into two subgroups and assign one subgroup the topic of LONELINESS and the other SOLITUDE.

6. Distribute one large sheet of paper to each subgroup, also providing a wide variety of markers, crayons, colored pencils and paints.

7. Instruct each subgroup to create a mural depicting their assigned topic.

8. Reconvene as a large group and facilitate discussion of each mural.

9. Display murals on a bulletin board, emphasizing healthy coping skill development.

10. Process benefits of this activity.

Journal Keeping

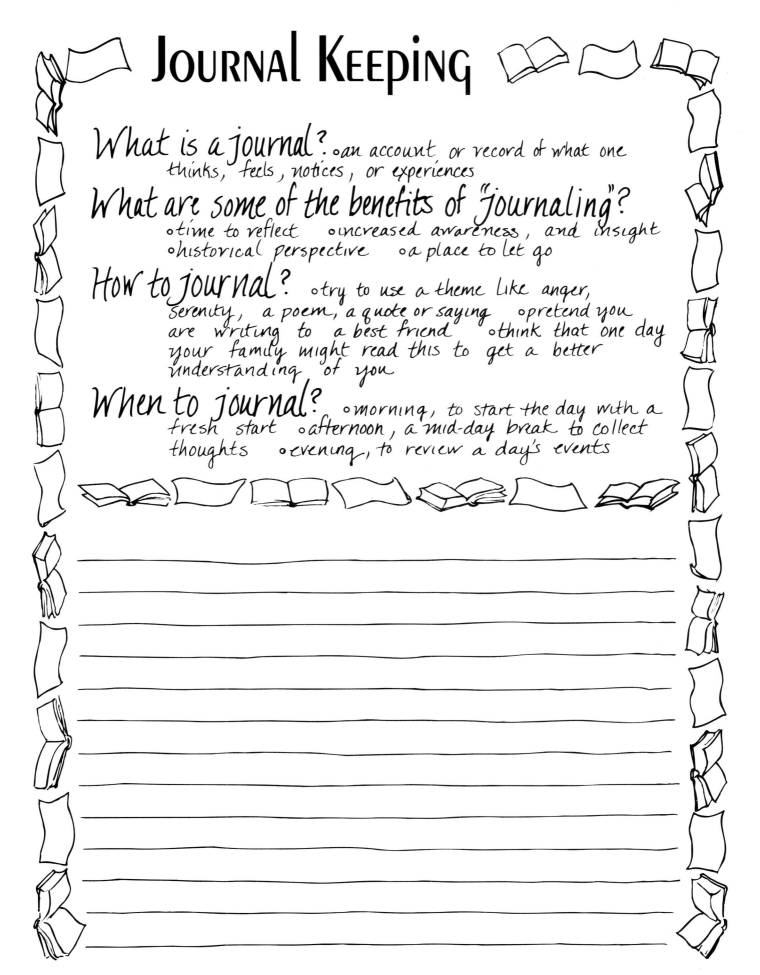

What is a journal? ○an account, or record of what one thinks, feels, notices, or experiences

What are some of the benefits of "journaling"?
○time to reflect   ○increased awareness, and insight   ○historical perspective   ○a place to let go

How to journal? ○try to use a theme like anger, serenity, a poem, a quote or saying   ○pretend you are writing to a best friend   ○think that one day your family might read this to get a better understanding of you

When to journal? ○morning, to start the day with a fresh start   ○afternoon, a mid-day break to collect thoughts   ○evening, to review a day's events

Journal Keeping

I. PURPOSE:

To increase coping skills by learning how to journal.

II. GENERAL COMMENTS:

Learning to journal is an inexpensive and very effective way of coping. It is a unique coping skill in that it can be done individually, it can be looked at by others (friends, family, professionals) at a later date, and is always a "safe place" to reveal one's true self. Like any new skill, it requires practice on a daily basis to be effective.

III. POSSIBLE ACTIVITIES:

A. 1. Introduce topic of journaling to group using above general comments as a guide.

2. Distribute handout allowing discussion of top half, encouraging group to offer their experiences and insights.

3. Set a realistic goal for group members to practice journaling, e.g., for three days. Photocopy entire handout 2 times, then cut off bottom portions and put together to make one 8-1/2" x 11" sheet. Photocopy this new sheet as many times as needed for all group members. Distribute correct number of journal sheets and staple together.

4. Reconvene, if possible, with group members as a group or individually, to discuss the "benefits" experienced with journaling, the "how-to" hints that worked, and the journaling that was most effective.

5. Process potential benefits and "trouble shoot" as necessary for effective journal keeping.

B. 1. Introduce topic of journaling to group using above general comments as a guide.

2. Distribute handout allowing discussion of top half, encouraging group to offer their experiences and insights.

3. Choose a theme that is common to the particular group right now, e.g., coping skills, grief/loss, anger, codependency, time management, communication skills, etc.

4. Ask group members to practice journal writing (within this identified theme), focusing on a situation that occurred during the past three days.

5. Allow 10 minutes to complete. Instruct members to pair off to share responses and to get feedback from partner for 5-10 minutes.

6. Encourage partners to share, if they are comfortable, the content of what they wrote, however to focus primarily on the process of journaling an event.

7. Reconvene as a large group to share insights and summarize information.

8. Give seven journal sheets (stapled together) as a homework assignment to each group member to be discussed next week on a 1:1 basis. (Photocopy entire handout 2 times, then cut off bottom portions and put together to make one 8-1/2" x 11" sheet. Photocopy this new sheet as many times as needed for all group members.)

9. Process benefits of this activity.

Poetry Power

Poetry can be used to unlock your creative voice and energy. It can be a way of communicating with yourself and with others. A way of mending and healing, that can be insightful, passionate and revealing.

Here are three examples of poetry:

by a 14 year-old writing to her friend after her friend's father passed away

> You ask why
> he was taken away
>
> God has his reasons
> even if they are strange.
>
> Your heart will heal
> but it will take time
> just pray a lot
> and you should be fine.

by a 35 year-old man reuniting with his love after eighteen years

> We were one stream.
> A cold, bright stream running
> swiftly from the north.
>
> At a rock we diverged.
> Water like the Tao
> chooses least resistance.
>
> Eighteen years later
> and much farther along
> We merged again
> before spilling into the ocean.

by a 44 year-old woman who is coping with early memories of abuse

> When I write
> I am trying to learn
> who I am,
> where I came from,
> where I am going.
>
> I write
> from darkness to darkness,
> but I'd never
> give up writing.
>
> It helps me know
> what I am capable of.
> I love the language
> for letting me learn.
>
> I write
> to know even the most painful
> memories. I write
> to tell the secrets
> and then to see
> that I can survive
> the telling.
>
> I write
> to be, to know, to think,
> to see, to understand.
>
> I write
> to learn
> to stay alive.

Now . . . explore new worlds:

_____
_____
_____
_____
_____
_____
_____
_____
_____
_____

_____

Poetry Power

I. PURPOSE:

To increase creative expression by exploring poetry.

II. GENERAL COMMENTS:

Poetry has been used throughout history as a method of self-understanding and healing. The therapeutic value of poetry can be to clarify thoughts, offer a safe place for self-expression, assist in grief work, give a message of hope, etc., etc., etc.! Professionals interested in pursuing their knowledge of poetry therapy should contact:

> The National Association for Poetry Therapy
> P.O. Box 551
> Port Washington, New York 11050

III. POSSIBLE ACTIVITIES:

A. 1. Distribute handouts and read aloud.

2. List on chalkboard possible benefits to poetry-writing.

3. Describe potential themes for poetry: feelings or mood, someone, an event.

4. Give group 10-15 minutes to write a poem on their handout.

5. Encourage volunteers to read theirs aloud, asking group members to be supportive and non-judgmental. Allow for discussion of "what moved you in the poem?"

6. Process benefits of poetry and this exercise.

B. 1. Distribute handouts and read aloud.

2. List on chalkboard possible benefits to poetry-writing.

3. Describe potential themes for poetry: feelings or mood, someone, an event.

4. Give group 10-15 minutes to write a poem on their handout.

5. Distribute large sheets of white paper and a variety of watercolors to each group member.

6. Ask group members to illustrate their poems through the use of watercolors, emphasizing that technique is not as important as symbolizing through colors, strokes, etc.

7. Encourage each member to share his/her poem(s), while displaying his/her painting(s), and facilitate support and feedback from others.

8. Process benefits of this creative expression activity.

Wellness Reproductions Inc. will publish a poetry anthology submitted by individuals involved in the therapeutic process. Possible areas of inclusion are: grief/loss, personal change and growth, relationships, etc. If interested, please submit to:

Wellness Reproductions Inc.
23945 Mercantile Rd.
Beachwood, OH 44122-5924

LET THE SUNSHINE IN

LET THE SUN SHINE IN

I. **PURPOSE:**

To improve the feedback skill of identifying positive traits in others.

To increase self-esteem.

II. **GENERAL COMMENTS:**

This activity allows the participants an opportunity to constructively express positive feelings for others, while learning how to graciously accept compliments. (It is important that all participants can read and write and are familiar with one another.)

III. **POSSIBLE ACTIVITIES:**

A. 1. Introduce the importance of positive feedback from peers and how feedback impacts self-esteem. Define self-esteem as a group.

2. With the group sitting in a circle or around a table, distribute one handout to each participant.

3. Each participant writes his/her name in the center of the sun.

4. The artwork is then passed to the person on the right who writes one positive comment about that person in a sunbeam.

5. The papers continue to rotate around the circle until each person writes about every other person in the group.

6. Once the sun is returned, instruct the participants to write a positive self-statement in the center of the sun.

7. Each participant takes a turn reading aloud all of his/her sunbeams.

8. The finished handouts can be hung in the participants' rooms or in an activity area, if appropriate, as a reminder of positive attributes.

9. Process the activity to see if the participants:

– were able to give and accept compliments?

– were able to be original on the different sunbeams?; or

– were the compliments set and routine?

B. 1. Define feedback for the group.

2. With the group sitting in a circle or around a table, distribute one handout to each participant.

3. Each participant writes his/her name in the center of the sun.

4. The artwork is then passed to the person on the right who writes one positive comment in a sunbeam.

5. The papers continue to rotate around the circle until each person writes about every other person in the group.

6. Once the sun is returned, instruct the participants to write a positive self-statement in the center of the sun.

7. Each participant takes a turn reading aloud all of his/her sunbeams.

8. Develop the theme of "sunshine" by listing on the chalkboard hot or warm things - fire, fireplace, hot soup, summer beach, sunbeams, bath, shower, hot chocolate, etc. Make a unit collage of these ideas emphasizing that positive feedback from others can also give a warm feeling.

9. Process by discussing how positive feedback can be used in day-to-day life and how it affects self-esteem.

Activity handout and facilitator's information adapted from submission by Lori Rosenberg, CTRS, University Heights, OH.

One of the most difficult **communication techniques** is to actively listen when receiving feedback.

Here are some active strategies to use:

STAGE I: Prepare Yourself
    a. Learn to recognize the "forerunners" of feedback, e.g., "I have something to talk to you about."
    b. Use self-talk or positive self-statements, e.g., "There's always room for improvements."
    c. Get ready to actively listen for potential growth.
    d. Be aware of body language.

STAGE II: Listen
    a. What behavior or action is being discussed?
    b. What changes are desired?
    c. Are there enough "specifics" to make changes?

STAGE III: Clarify
    a. Ask questions to get more information as needed.
    b. Restate feedback as you understand it.

STAGE IV: Evaluate Information
    a. What are the qualifications of the message-giver?
    b. Have I heard this information before?
    c. Is this feedback relevant to me?

STAGE V: Make Decisions
    a. Am I willing to make desired changes?
    b. What do I have to lose? What do I have to gain?
    c. What is my chance of succeeding? Am I willing to take the chance?
    d. How much time and energy will it take to make these changes?
    e. Are there compromises that can be made?

NOTES

SET THE STAGE

I. PURPOSE:

To increase communication skills by becoming aware of active strategies for receiving feedback.

II. GENERAL COMMENTS:

There are many "blocks" used when receiving feedback – denial, defending, avoiding, attacking, etc. To be an effective communicator, one needs the skill of listening well to feedback that is being offered. Breaking the process into specific, approachable steps can be helpful when learning new strategies.

III. POSSIBLE ACTIVITIES:

A. 1. Distribute handouts and review.

2. Practice with role-plays the group suggests or the following:

   a. boss offers feedback on job performance

   b. spouse offers feedback on cooking / cleaning / maintaining home ability

   c. friend offers feedback on interpersonal skills

   d. father / mother offers feedback on method of raising children

   e. sister / brother offers feedback on role in family

3. Appoint 2-3 group members the role of reminding or cueing the "receiver" as to the outlined stages and strategies.

4. Evaluate and process each role-play, reminding group members that these skills need to be acquired through hard work and practice.

5. Process the group by asking group members how they can benefit from information presented during this group.

B. 1. Discuss topic of receiving feedback by reviewing handout, asking group members for their immediate emotional reactions to the topic.

2. Encourage group members to write down on strips of paper two situations in which they received feedback that was difficult for them.

3. Gather all strips of paper in a bowl and mix together.

4. Taking turns, have group members choose one situation (not their own) from the bowl and state how they would respond.

5. Encourage role-plays of the most difficult ones.

6. Process the benefits of this activity.

CREATIVE EXERCISING

SOCK HOP & SQUEEZE

Roll up 1 or 2 pair of socks. Use in exercises to strengthen hands and arms. "Twist", "Squeeze", "Flexes", "Washboard scrubs" . . . .

JUGGERSIZES

Fill empty milk containers with water or sand to fit your capabilities and/or level of strength. (Sitting, standing, or lying down.)

U-CAN-DO IT

Take two small canned-good items to lift during exercises.

WHIP IT GOOD

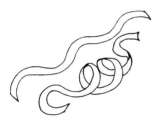

Cut bright colored strips of crepe paper, lace, or ribbon or use scarves, handkerchieves, etc. Then invent movements to recorded music or radio. Use your imagination! "Twist", "Shake your boa", "Crazy 8's", "Whip & pull", "Lift & snake", "Circles".

HANDLE WITH FLARE

Use broom handle, 1" dowel, or sturdy cane. Lift, twist and even pump weights when combined with "Juggersizes". (Put stick through handles.)

SPLISH-SPLASH STRETCH

Using a regular bath towel, do various stretch & pull exercises. Can also put towel through handle of milk jugs to vary weight & exercises.

JARRIN' LOOSE

Fill two small plastic peanut butter jars with popcorn, beans, or colored buttons. As exercise movements are performed there will be lots of sound!

EXERCISING CAN BE FUN!

CREATIVE EXERCISING

I. **PURPOSE:**

To increase fitness through creative exercising that can be done at home, alone, and inexpensively.

II. **GENERAL COMMENTS:**

Creative and inexpensive exercise programs are often used for inpatients or outpatients, and then recommended for home use. Most suggested items can be found in the clinic or home, and are easy to adapt to meet individual's needs.

III. **POSSIBLE ACTIVITIES:**

A. 1. Prepare for group by collecting required exercise supplies.

2. Arrange chairs in circle.

3. Use handout to recommend exercises. Do 2 sets if group members are able, to reinforce learning new exercises. Have fun with radio or cassette tapes.

4. Distribute handouts, recommending that these exercises be done at least 3 times weekly.

5. Ask an individual to process the group by outlining the benefits of exercise.

B. 1. Prepare for group by collecting required exercise supplies, and arranging chairs in a circle.

2. Photocopy one handout per group member and prior to group, highlight a different exercise on each copy.

3. Distribute copies to all group members and draw their attention to the one exercise highlighted on their individual copies.

4. Ask each group member to take turns leading the exercise highlighted on his/her handout, with group leader's assistance on 1st set and on own during 2nd set. Have fun with radio or cassette tapes!

5. Continue until all group members have had a turn co-leading/leading, and all exercises have been done 2 times.

6. Ask an individual to process the group by outlining the benefits of exercise. Recommend that these exercises be done 3 times minimum per week to maintain fitness.

Activity handout, illustrations, and facilitator's information submitted by Joeleau Harl, RT, Keokuk, IA.

FEELING FIT

FEELING FIT TAKES A **PROACTIVE APPROACH** TO EDUCATING YOURSELF ON SOME OF THE BASIC COMPONENTS OF FITNESS.

AEROBIC

Over the past few years, a general consensus was reached about the basic aerobic conditioning program an average individual should maintain in order to be fit. A fitness program should include an aerobic activity like stair-climbing, cross-country skiing, or running. Working out three to four times weekly will help one attain and maintain his/her optimum fitness level. Each session should be between 20 to 40 minutes.

In order not to undertrain or overtrain, it is important to know how to figure maximum heart rate and target heart rate zone. It is recommended to exercise within the target heart rate zone for a minimum of 20 minutes. One of the basic formulas is as follows:

EXAMPLE: for a 30-year old

```
      220
  –    30   (age)
      190   maximum heart rate
  x   .80
      152   upper limit of target zone
- - - - - - - - - - - - - - - - - - -
      190   maximum heart rate
  x   .60
      114   lower limit of target zone
```

This formula is intended for the general fitness user. One should consult a physician before starting any aerobic fitness program.

NUTRITION

Nutrition is a significant part of any fitness program, as well as an important contributor to an overall healthy lifestyle. A daily diet consisting of a variety of fresh fruit and vegetables, carbohydrates (whole grain breads and cereals), dairy products, and protein sources is recommended. Low fat, low sugar, low sodium, and low cholesterol are important guidelines for eating nutritiously.

STRENGTH & FLEXIBILITY

Strength and flexibility are also important aspects of any fitness program.

STRENGTH
Weight training using either free weights or machines is an effective way to increase muscle strength. While there are many schools of thought regarding weight training, for the novice it is best to talk to an athletic trainer found at most gyms or community colleges about specific routines.

FLEXIBILITY
Deals with the range of motion of the joints and muscles an individual can exhibit. Stretching is an important contributing factor in flexibility. To avoid an injury, a rule of thumb is that warm muscles are less likely to sustain injury than cold ones. If, for instance, the sport of choice is tennis, one way of warming up would be to gently and slowly go through all the motions one would anticipate making during a regular match. Once a light sweat is rendered, one can then participate vigorously.

MY FITNESS PLAN

AEROBIC	NUTRITION	STRENGTH & FLEXIBILITY
_____	_____	_____
_____	_____	_____
_____	_____	_____
_____	_____	_____
_____	_____	_____
_____	_____	_____
_____	_____	_____

FEELING FIT

I. PURPOSE:

To increase healthy living by addressing three components of fitness: aerobic, strength & flexibility, and nutrition.

II. GENERAL COMMENTS:

Staying and keeping healthy requires knowledge, understanding, and determination. Three basic components of fitness are outlined so that individual fitness plans can be developed.

III. POSSIBLE ACTIVITIES:

A. 1. Review all content material.

2. Brainstorm on chalkboard aerobic activities and exercises to increase strength and flexibility. Continue with listing one to two healthy meals.

3. Ask all group members to develop written individual fitness plans.

4. Share plans.

5. Process benefits of this activity.

B. 1. Divide group into three subgroups.

2. Ask each subgroup to read over one section (aerobic, strength & flexibility, or nutrition), and in five minutes list as many ideas or suggestions they can think of in this category.

For example - Aerobics:

Step-aerobics	Mountain climbing
Swimming	Tennis
Running	Bicycling
Jogging	Racquetball
Hiking	Volleyball
Fast walking	Basketball
Stair-climbing	Soccer
Dancercize	Baseball
Treadmilling	

3. Bring the group together again to share ideas.

4. Give group five minutes to complete individual fitness plans. Divide group into pairs to share.

5. Process benefits of this activity, and offer additional resources (books, audiotapes, videotapes, community centers, classes, etc.) as suggestions for further follow-up.

Activity handout and facilitator's information submitted by Siri-Dya S. Khalsa, M.Ed., Hudson, OH.

I·N·N·E·R VOICE

Within each of us is a wisdom, a "knowing", a voice of intuition, a conscience, a still, small inner-voice — our spirit — that can guide us, if we allow it. How can we go about nurturing our spirit? By becoming quiet and achieving a stillness – you'll get a general sense about what your inner-voice is telling you.

Check off and write in what might work for you, in order to become relaxed, slow down your thoughts, and enjoy solitude.

_____ leisurely walks	_____ self-affirmations	_____ running / jogging
_____ meditation	_____ poetry writing	_____ journal writing
_____ exercise	_____ nature	_____ imagining
_____ music	_____ prayer	_____ long ride
_____ art work	_____ day-dreaming	_____ visualization
_____ photography	_____ relaxing bath / shower	_____ inspirational books
_____ _____	_____ _____	_____ _____
_____ _____	_____ _____	_____ _____

Allow your inner-voice to speak to you – through thoughts, funny feelings / sensations, hunches, impulses, gut feelings, dreams, or other body reactions. Finding our inner-voice takes courage, perseverance, and faith. Listen carefully. Act upon it with guidance from someone you trust. To make sure that your voice from within is on the right track, list three people that can listen to you and will give you honest feedback. Responding to your inner-voice will help you hear it even stronger in the future.

1. _____   2. _____   3. _____

> ### CONNECTING OURSELVES TO OUR INNER-VOICE BRINGS INNER-PEACE, HEALTHY CHOICES AND SPIRITUAL SUPPORT.

INNER-VOICE

I. PURPOSE:

To improve healthy living by increasing awareness of one's inner-voice and the impact it can have on one's life.

II. GENERAL COMMENTS:

In today's society, people are so often distracted by increasingly busy lives, that they are drawn away from their spiritual selves. Learning to listen to one's inner-voice and, with guidance, to act on it, will help bring a focus back to healthy living.

To quote Dr. O. Carl Simonton of the Simonton Cancer Center, "Surprisingly, the most health-supporting emotional state seems not to be enthusiasm or even optimism, but serenity and peacefulness. In addition to exploring the role of the mind in promoting health, I believe it's equally important to consider the role of the *spirit*. When we're aware of the spiritual dimension of life, we have access to many powerful resources that aren't available when we limit our focus to mind and body. It isn't necessary to practice a *particular* religion – or to hold any special theological views – in order to embrace the concept of spirituality. The dictionary refers to spirit as life principle . . . the force that gives us vitality, drives and motivates us, and supports our survival."

It is important to note that the inner-voice referred to on this handout is not hallucinatory in nature, and that group members need to be carefully chosen for inclusion in this activity.

III. POSSIBLE ACTIVITIES:

A. 1. Distribute handouts and discuss with group members.

2. Instruct all group members to complete handout.

3. Share as able with discussion of additional ideas for how to get in touch with one's inner-voice.

4. Emphasize importance of seeking support to be certain that one's inner-voice is on the right track.

5. Process benefits of this activity.

B. 1. Discuss concept of inner-voice and ask group members to share personal experiences.

2. Distribute handout, asking group members to first complete top portion of handout.

3. On reverse side of handout, ask group members to visually represent (1) an experience where they heard their inner-voice; (2) how their inner-voice feels to them; or (3) how it looks to them.

4. Encourage creativity and free expression with this abstract concept.

5. Discuss similarities and differences of individuals' perceptions by comparing colors, shapes, sizes, images, etc., which symbolize their inner-voices.

6. Encourage group members to complete bottom portion of the handout, emphasizing the importance of seeking support to be certain that one's inner-voice is on the right track.

7. Process benefits of this activity and discuss how group members can develop the capacity to trust their inner-voices.

ASK WENDY

Statistics indicate that more and more women are entering and re-entering the workforce. The benefits of working outside of the home extend far beyond the obvious financial advantages. Many women have found that the areas in their lives that improved while employed were: self-esteem, sense of belonging, competence, independence, and time effectiveness, among others. The great challenge, however, is to achieve balance and to avoid falling into the "superwoman syndrome".

The following are typical questions from women entering and re-entering the workforce, with some answers from our workplace specialist, Wendy! She gives you *some* information, and the rest is for you to fill in!

Q: **"I'm looking for a job, but don't know where to start. Can you give me a few tips?"**

A: Try the following ideas . . .

- Networking and word-of-mouth (80-85% of jobs are acquired this way!). Say to friends, family, former employers, co-workers, neighbors, acquaintances, "If you hear of any job openings, _____ _____ _____."

(fill in – be creative!)

- Newspaper and classified ads
- Magazines and journals
- Job fairs
- *Hitting the pavement* (door-to-door contacts)
- _____
- _____
- _____

Q: **"Which work skills do employers consider the most valuable?"**

A: This varies from job to job, but generally speaking, the most valuable are:

- Knowledgeable and trainable for job desired
- Dependable
- Honest and assertive communication
- Organized
- Loyal
- Positive personality

- Time-effective
- Resourceful
- Genuine interest in company
- Willing to offer suggestions and ideas
- _____
- _____
- _____

Q: **"I'm starting a new job in two weeks . . . what are specific characteristics or behaviors that employers <u>don't</u> like?"**

A: Here's just a few:

- Poor time management - arriving late, procrastinating, difficulty with setting priorities for self, inability to delegate when needed

- Gossip or badmouthing other employees
- *Just putting in my time* attitude
- Non-assertive communication skills
- _____
- _____

Ask Wendy

I. PURPOSE:

To increase knowledge of pertinent job readiness information.

II. GENERAL COMMENTS:

As mentioned on the front of the handout, more and more women are entering and re-entering the workforce. Oftentimes, women may not be in tune to the job seeking-and-finding process, as well as to the characteristics that many employers look for <u>and</u> discourage in their employees. This Q & A format allows individuals to take a look at several important points to consider when they are ready to start job-hunting.

III. POSSIBLE ACTIVITIES:

A. 1. Distribute handouts to group members and discuss opening paragraph.

2. Facilitate additional discussion related to group members' experiences or lack of experiences with employment.

3. As a group, review questions #1-3 on handout, and "Wendy's" responses, encouraging group members to fill in the blanks as appropriate.

4. Process group by asking members to identify benefits of this activity.

B. 1. Distribute handouts to group members and discuss opening paragraph.

2. Facilitate additional discussion related to group members' experiences or lack of experiences with employment.

3. As a group, review questions #1-3 on handout, and "Wendy's" responses, encouraging group members to fill in the blanks as appropriate.

4. Ask group to divide into triads for further work in this topic.

5. Instruct each triad to identify 1-3 additional questions (depending on time allotment) that they have regarding entering/re-entering the workforce, and to write them on a separate piece of paper provided by group facilitator.

6. Collect all papers from triads and redistribute them, so that triads do not receive the same set of questions which they wrote.

7. Encourage each triad to problem-solve answers to these job-readiness questions and share them with large group when everyone has finished.

8. Provide additional job-readiness information as needed to facilitate thorough discussion.

9. Process benefits of this activity.

GETTING READY FOR WORK?

Considering entering or re-entering the workplace? Here is an overview of the job preparation process.

Check off the appropriate boxes and fill in the blanks.

Y ☐ N ☐ **1. I know what kind of job I'm looking for (geographical location, level of responsibility, pay, working conditions, environment/people, etc.).**

If no, what information do I need and where can I find it? _____

_____

If yes, describe the details and characteristics: _____

_____

Y ☐ N ☐ **2. I know how to discover potential employers in the area and network (friends, family, newspapers, magazines, former colleagues, etc.).**

If no, how can I learn to network? _____

_____

If yes, list potential employers to contact: _____

_____

_____

Y ☐ N ☐ **3. I know how to write a résumé.**

If no, where can I learn this skill? _____

_____

If yes, list 2-3 people I can show my résumé to in order to get feedback.

_____

_____

Y ☐ N ☐ **4. I know how to write a cover letter.**

If no, where can I learn this skill? _____

_____

If yes, list 2-3 people I can show my cover letter to in order to get feedback.

_____

_____

When you're able to answer "yes" to all 4 questions, you'll be ready to make contacts and set-up interviews!!

Good Luck!

GETTING READY FOR WORK?

I. PURPOSE:

To increase job readiness by reviewing need for making decisions, for networking, and for writing résumés and cover letters.

II. GENERAL COMMENTS:

Adequate job readiness requires several skills. A few are indicated on this handout to allow people who are considering entering or re-entering the workplace, to get on the right track.

III. POSSIBLE ACTIVITIES:

A. 1. Distribute handouts.

    2. Explain that "getting ready for work" includes adequate job preparation.

    3. Review handout, as explained on front, together as a group.

    4. Bring to group additional resources to review, such as sample cover letters or résumés, books, articles on topics discussed, classified ads, etc. Offer specific information as needed, e.g., #4—cover letter—purpose, design and hints such as explaining gaps in employment history, emphasis of previous work skills, as well as activities and skills developed during off-time from work.

    5. Encourage dyads or triads to meet for 5-10 minutes to help one another with ideas, or for skill-building.

    6. Process benefits of this activity and ask each group member, "What is the next step you can take in order to get the skills you need to get a job?"

B. 1. Distribute handouts.

    2. Brainstorm on chalkboard and discuss a list of areas which need to be addressed when preparing to enter/re-enter the workforce, e.g., interviewing skills, résumé writing, setting-up childcare arrangements, etc.

    3. Distribute handouts and review as a group.

    4. Encourage group members to complete.

    5. Practice role-playing interview situations, giving each group member an opportunity to be "interviewed".

    6. Process benefits of job preparation/job readiness skills.

1 WEEK OF PRESENTS

MONDAY _____

_____
_____
_____
_____
_____
_____

TUESDAY _____

_____
_____
_____
_____
_____
_____

WEDNESDAY _____

_____
_____
_____
_____
_____

THURSDAY _____

_____
_____
_____
_____
_____

FRIDAY _____

_____
_____
_____
_____

SATURDAY _____

_____
_____
_____

SUNDAY _____

_____
_____

1 WEEK OF PRESENTS

I. PURPOSE:

To increase self-esteem by planning to give oneself a week of presents as a celebration of one's own uniqueness.

II. GENERAL COMMENTS:

Everyone likes to celebrate and be celebrated. An important skill to have is the ability to give oneself worthwhile presents. They can vary in size, cost, shape, etc., and be material or non-material, but they must have great "value" and, like all meaningful gifts, require careful thought.

III. POSSIBLE ACTIVITIES:

A. 1. Discuss the value of presents: what qualities do "treasured gifts" have?

2. Ask the group to consider what it would be like to receive 1 gift a day for 7 days. How would that affect ones self-esteem?

3. Distribute handouts. Provide if necessary a limited number of examples, e.g.,

   a. give myself $1/2$ hour of workout time, hobby/craft time
   b. buy myself a new computer game, jigsaw puzzle, book, etc.
   c. buy fresh flowers
   d. go to a bookstore and buy 1 book
   e. take a nap

4. Encourage group members to be personal and unique, giving themselves presents that are meaningful to them.

5. Ask group members to complete their handout by considering their individual schedules as they fill out 1 week of presents.

6. Share as a group, the variety of responses.

7. Process how gift-giving to oneself can increase self-esteem.

B. 1. Discuss the value of "presents": what qualities do "treasured gifts" have?

2. Brainstorm on chalkboard a list of "presents" that group members would like to receive, emphasizing that "presents" do not <u>always</u> mean material objects. Give an example of a non-material gift, e.g., $1/2$ hour of "alone-time".

3. Distribute handouts and ask all group members to complete by identifying 1 "present" each day they can give to themselves with at least $1/2$ of them being non-material gifts.

4. Discuss as a group, reviewing how giving oneself "presents" can increase self-esteem. Discuss any differences members feel between material and non-material gifts.

5. Encourage members to place their completed handout in a conspicuous place, e.g., refrigerator, bulletin board, purse/wallet.

6. Process benefits of this activity.

REWARD yourself!

How often do you feel this ⟩ way? You are not alone! Many men in today's society experience feelings of stress, fatigue, career burnout, and lack of connectedness. A reason for this might be the increase in the number of roles as well as the increase in the responsibilities within these roles.

What are your current roles?

☐ Husband   ☐ Father   ☐ Grandfather
☐ Brother   ☐ Uncle   ☐ Step-father
☐ Grandson   ☐ Father-in-law   ☐ Employee
☐ Son   ☐ Money manager   ☐ Home owner
☐ Employer   ☐ Single parent   ☐ Student
☐ Provider   ☐ Home maintainer   ☐ Boyfriend
☐ Volunteer   ☐ _____   ☐ _____

<u>NOW</u> is the time to do something for yourself!

What can you do to *REWARD yourself?*

List 3 ways you can reward yourself for working so hard.

5 MINUTES	15 MINUTES	30 (+) MINUTES
Examples: _____ _____ _____ _____ Favorite: _____	Examples: _____ _____ _____ _____ Favorite: _____	Examples: _____ _____ _____ _____ Favorite: _____

I. **PURPOSE:**

To identify increased role responsibilities and recognize possible self-rewards.

II. **GENERAL COMMENTS:**

Roles have changed with increasing responsibilities for today's men. Traditional male roles (i.e. father, provider) are now surrounded by the demands of other roles (i.e. single parent, husband); this leaves many men exhausted and overwhelmed. Men, in general, lack quality time for themselves. Finding ways to "reward" oneself for hard work may be used as a coping skill. In addition, it will also give one the "vitalized" feeling needed to continue one's important work.

III. **POSSIBLE ACTIVITIES:**

A. 1. Distribute handouts.

2. Instruct all group members to complete top half of handout.

3. Brainstorm on chalkboard examples of self-rewards, e.g., 5 minutes - enjoy silence; 15 minutes - listen to music; 30 (+) minutes - exercise or pursue a hobby.

4. Continue this activity by instructing the group members to write down the self-rewards that are of interest to them in the appropriate slots stated on the handout.

5. Encourage group members to discuss what they will do for "self-rewards" on an ongoing basis.

6. Process the benefits of this activity.

B. 1. Distribute handouts.

2. Provide group members with magazines (preferably with men's topics).

3. Ask group members to look for pictures or articles that represent self-rewards or "treats".

4. Encourage group members to share with one another the self-rewards or treats they found. Write them in the appropriate boxes.

5. Instruct group members to choose their favorite and share with the group.

6. Ask group members to piece and then glue cut-outs together for a unit collage or bulletin board.

7. Process the benefits of this activity.

Activity handout and facilitator's information adapted from submission by
Teresa A. Bachtel, COTA/L, Barberton, OH. and Siri-Dya S. Khalsa, M.Ed., Hudson, OH.

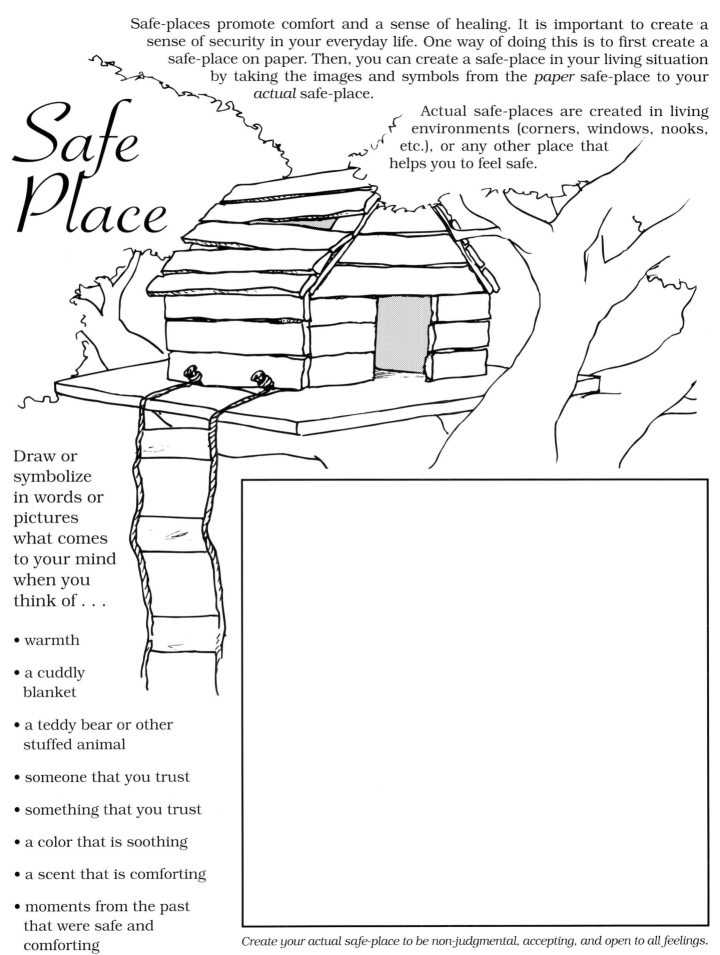

Safe-places promote comfort and a sense of healing. It is important to create a sense of security in your everyday life. One way of doing this is to first create a safe-place on paper. Then, you can create a safe-place in your living situation by taking the images and symbols from the *paper* safe-place to your *actual* safe-place.

Actual safe-places are created in living environments (corners, windows, nooks, etc.), or any other place that helps you to feel safe.

Safe Place

Draw or symbolize in words or pictures what comes to your mind when you think of . . .

- warmth

- a cuddly blanket

- a teddy bear or other stuffed animal

- someone that you trust

- something that you trust

- a color that is soothing

- a scent that is comforting

- moments from the past that were safe and comforting

Create your actual safe-place to be non-judgmental, accepting, and open to all feelings.

Safe-Place

I. PURPOSE:

To nurture oneself by promoting comfort and a sense of healing.

II. GENERAL COMMENTS:

Some people have memories/pain/abuse from their past that affect their everyday life. Creating imaginary safe-places will be a beginning to developing real safe-places in personal living situations.

III. POSSIBLE ACTIVITIES:

A. 1. Distribute handouts and read aloud entire page to grasp concept.

2. List on a chalkboard things that come to mind when "teddy bear" is mentioned. Continue with other points of what to include.

3. Ask each group member to draw with images, symbols or words what belongs in his/her safe-place.

4. Share, as above, in the group.

5. Plan with group members how they can create a safe-place in their homes, discussing benefits.

B. 1. Distribute handouts and read aloud entire page to grasp concept.

2. Ask each group member to draw with images, symbols or words what belongs in his/her safe-place.

3. Distribute large sheets of construction paper to each group member. Make available a variety of magazines, scissors, and glue to all members.

4. Instruct all members to further develop their safe-places by making a magazine picture collage.

5. Discuss as a group each member's paper safe-place and collage safe-place, and encourage sharing of ideas for creating a safe-place in each member's living environment.

6. Process benefits of this activity.

Activity handout adapted from idea submitted by Karen Templeton, RN, Montrose, PA.

TREAT yourself!

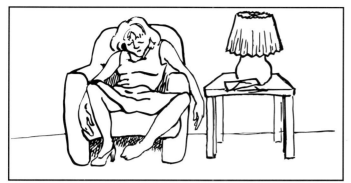 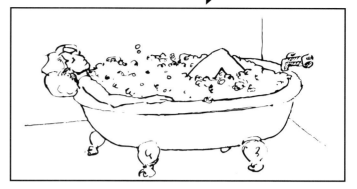

How often do you feel this way? You are not alone! Many women in today's society are experiencing feelings of stress, fatigue, multiple-role burnout, and lack of emotional nurturance. A reason for this might be the increase in the number of roles, as well as the increase in the responsibilities within these roles.

What are your current roles?

☐ Wife	☐ Mother	☐ Daughter
☐ Sister	☐ Aunt	☐ Grandmother
☐ Granddaughter	☐ Mother-in-law	☐ Step-mother
☐ Step-daughter	☐ Sister-in-law	☐ Employee
☐ Employer	☐ Money manager	☐ Homemaker
☐ Caregiver	☐ Single parent	☐ Student
☐ Volunteer	☐ _____	☐ _____

<u>NOW</u> is the time to do something for yourself!

What can you do to *TREAT yourself?*

List 3 ways you can reward yourself for working so hard.

5 MINUTES	**15 MINUTES**	**30 (+) MINUTES**
Examples: _____ _____ _____ _____ Favorite: _____	Examples: _____ _____ _____ _____ Favorite: _____	Examples: _____ _____ _____ _____ Favorite: _____

TREAT yourself!

I. **PURPOSE:**

To identify increased role responsibilities and recognize possible self-rewards.

II. **GENERAL COMMENTS:**

Roles have changed with increasing responsibilities for today's women. Traditional female roles (i.e. mother, cook) are now surrounded by the demands of other roles (i.e. single parent, employee); this leaves many women exhausted and overwhelmed. Women, in general, lack quality time for themselves. Finding ways to "reward" oneself for hard work may be used as a coping skill. In addition, it will also give one the "vitalized" feeling needed to continue one's important work.

III. **POSSIBLE ACTIVITIES:**

A. 1. Distribute handouts.

2. Instruct all group members to complete top half of handout.

3. Brainstorm on chalkboard examples of self-rewards, e.g., 5 minutes - paint fingernails; 15 minutes - soak in hot bubble bath; 30 (+) minutes - invite a friend over for tea / coffee / juice.

4. Continue this activity by instructing the group members to write down the self-rewards that are of interest to them in the appropriate slots stated on the handout.

5. Encourage group members to discuss what they will do for "self-rewards" on an ongoing basis.

6. Process the benefits of this activity.

B. 1. Distribute handouts.

2. Provide group members with magazines (preferably with women's topics).

3. Ask group members to look for pictures or articles that represent self-rewards or "treats".

4. Encourage group members to share with one another the self-rewards or treats they found. Write them in the appropriate boxes.

5. Instruct group members to choose their favorite and share with the group.

6. Ask group members to piece and then glue cut-outs together for a unit collage or bulletin board.

7. Process the benefits of this activity.

Activity handout and facilitator's information adapted from submission by Teresa A. Bachtel, COTA/L, Barberton, OH.

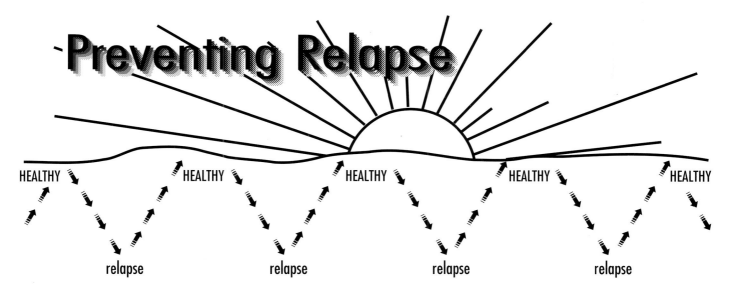

Preventing Relapse

RELAPSE, in the general sense, can be defined as a process of gradual decline in function which precedes or leads to the recurrence of a particular disease, illness or unhealthy behavior pattern. **RELAPSE** may occur with mental illness, chemical dependency, physical illness, and/or other health-related issues. **RELAPSE** is often preventable if individuals are aware of their symptoms/warning signs as they occur, and take charge by making specific changes.

Listed directly below are some possible symptoms/warning signs of **RELAPSE**. Check off those that apply to you and list the top five in the chart below. Then, identify your usual response to these symptoms/warning signs. Next, identify any changes you can make to address these. Finally, identify what significant others can do to support you when they recognize/notice one or more of your symptoms/warning signs are surfacing.

Possible Symptoms/Warning Signs of RELAPSE:

- depressive mood
- lack or loss of self-confidence
- denial of symptom onset
- poor judgement
- compulsive/impulsive behavior
- confusion
- difficulty making decisions
- easily irritated/angered

- unhealthy eating patterns
- lack of organization of daily routine
- feeling of helplessness
- unhealthy sleeping patterns
- use of substances to elevate mood
- apathy
- withdrawal from usual activities
- inability to concentrate/focus attention

When I Experience . . . (my symptom/warning sign)	I Usually . . . (my response)	In the Future, I Will Try . . . (my change/plan)	What My Significant Others Can Do To Help . . .
1.			
2.			
3.			
4.			
5.			

Preventing Relapse

I. **PURPOSE:**

To increase recognition of symptoms/warning signs of relapse.

To increase problem solving in relation to relapse prevention.

II. **GENERAL COMMENTS:**

This handout can be particularly helpful within the mental health and chemical dependency fields, although with some adaptations, could be used in other areas as well. Relapse prevention can be facilitated by recognizing symptoms/warning signs, planning, and seeking support from significant others. In this way, the cycle can usually be interrupted before the illness goes full-course again.

III. **POSSIBLE ACTIVITIES:**

A. 1. Distribute handouts to all group members and discuss opening paragraph and significance of graphics.

2. Instruct group members to complete both sections of handout.

3. Ask group members to share their top two responses with group, and facilitate support and feedback among members.

4. Make five photocopies of each member's bottom portion of handout. Suggest that they keep one to two copies in a conspicuous place for their own use, and give the remaining handouts to significant others who will support them.

5. Process benefits of this activity.

B. 1. Distribute handouts to all group members and discuss opening paragraph and significance of graphics.

2. Instruct group members to complete both sections of handout.

3. Taking turns, ask group members to choose one of their top symptoms/warning signs and do a role-play of *their usual response* and *what their significant other can do to help.*

4. Continue until all group members have had an opportunity to role-play one of their own situations.

5. Make five photocopies of each member's bottom portion of handout. Suggest that they keep one to two copies in a conspicuous place for their own use, and give the remaining handouts to significant others who will support them.

6. Process benefits of this activity and ask them to identify one of their significant others.

Road To Recovery

3. _____

2. _____

1. _____

The Road to Recovery certainly will not be a smooth one. Many obstacles, anticipated or not, will lie ahead. The key to not 'slipping' or 'relapsing' is to develop appropriate plans or coping skills to deal with these risky situations.

RISKY SITUATION #1: _____
How will I deal with it? _____
_____

RISKY SITUATION #2: _____
How will I deal with it? _____
_____

RISKY SITUATION #3: _____
How will I deal with it? _____
_____

I. **PURPOSE:**

To facilitate recovery by:
(1) recognizing potentially risky situations or relapse triggers, and
(2) identifying appropriate methods of coping with these situations.

To problem solve a plan of action.

II. **GENERAL COMMENTS:**

It is impossible to predict all the obstacles or risky situations one will encounter. However, if one does not possess the tools and the resources to deal with life's stresses, one tends to fall back on old, inappropriate methods of coping.

III. **POSSIBLE ACTIVITIES:**

A. 1. Distribute handouts.

2. Discuss topic of potentially risky situations.

3. Instruct each group member to identify 3 of their own high-risk situations.

4. Encourage each member to generate possible ways to handle or cope with each situation now that they are sober or non-using.

5. Discuss individuals' risky situations with the group and brainstorm other alternative methods of coping. Receive feedback from the group.

6. Process the importance/benefits of recognizing potentially risky situations before they happen.

B. 1. Distribute handouts.

2. Discuss topic of potentially risky situations.

3. Instruct each group member to identify 3 of their own high-risk situations.

4. Select a few risky situations from the group and role-play each one. Allow members of the group to practice their coping skills in simulated situations.

5. Allow group members to offer feedback and to help generate other possible methods of coping.

6. Process the importance of role-playing in order to practice their skills and their need to develop a plan of action.

Activity handout and facilitator's information adapted from submission by Christine Miccio, CTRS, Port St. Lucie, FL.

ENERGIZING vs. DRAINING

 VS.

SOME PEOPLE WE SPEND TIME WITH GIVE US ENERGY, WHILE OTHERS MAY drain US.

1. List the names of people you spend a lot of time with
   (at your job, in your family, socially, etc.).

2. NEXT TO EACH, jot down their attitudes and behaviors.

3. Then, determine if this person:
   energizes (E) you, drains (D) you, or has no effect (N/A) on you.

NAME	THEIR ATTITUDES / BEHAVIOR	E	D	N/A
1.				
2.				
3.				
4.				
5.				
6.				
7.				
8.				
9.				
10.				

GOALS Action Plan: _____

_____

_____

_____

ENERGIZING vs. DRAINING

I.   PURPOSE:

To improve conflict management by determining which relationships are "energizing" or "draining".

To develop an action plan to increase supportive relationships.

II.   GENERAL COMMENTS:

All relationships need to have a "give and take" quality. However, at times, certain relationships have a negative "draining" quality that does not promote wellness. Other relationships might promote an "energizing" quality. It is wise to evaluate all relationships, attempting to increase the energizing qualities of relationships, thereby creating a supportive environment.

III.   POSSIBLE ACTIVITIES:

A.   1.   Write "energize" and "drain" on the chalkboard.

2.   List with group members those factors in life that fall into each category, e.g.,

Energize = E	Drain = D
working out	money problems
successes at work	poor relationship with grandmother
loving children	arguments with children / parents / spouse
quiet dinners	frequent illness

Explain that today's group will focus on relationships.

3.   Distribute handouts, completing with names of those people that affect group members. Encourage a variety of sources, (e.g., friends, family, clergy, teachers, neighbors, acquaintances, long-distance relationships, etc.)

4.   Discuss results, establishing if there are any commonalities, differences or trends.

5.   Using this knowledge, facilitate the writing of action plans at the bottom, e.g., I will spend more time with my next door neighbor in the evenings.

6.   Process by sharing action plans.

B.   1.   Prior to group, prepare a deck of cards with an equal number of cards marked E (for energize) and D (for drain).

2.   Discuss with group members the energizing / draining concept and influence on relationships with others and self.

3.   Distribute handouts and instruct group members to complete.

4.   When completed, reconvene as a large group and ask members to take turns choosing cards.

5.   Instruct all members to discuss a person that energizes them, if they choose an "E" card, and a person that drains them, if they choose a "D" card.

6.   Encourage sharing of action plans.

7.   Process benefits of this activity.

BREAKING DOWN OUR WALLS

What attitudes and behaviors may get in the way of you forming or maintaining quality relationships?

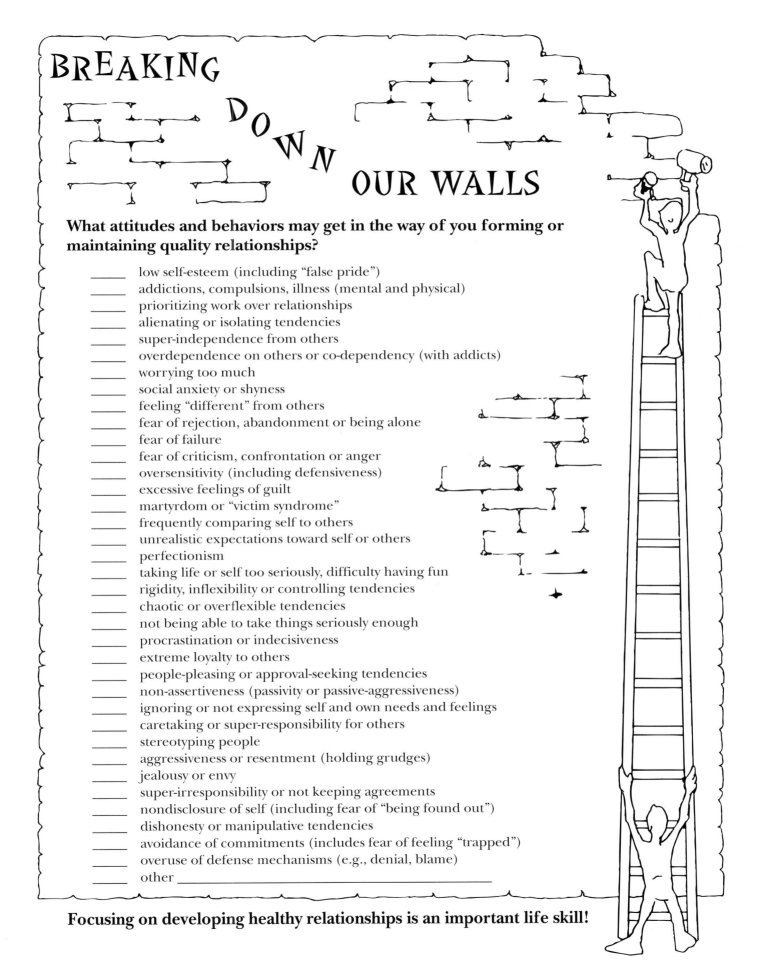

_____ low self-esteem (including "false pride")
_____ addictions, compulsions, illness (mental and physical)
_____ prioritizing work over relationships
_____ alienating or isolating tendencies
_____ super-independence from others
_____ overdependence on others or co-dependency (with addicts)
_____ worrying too much
_____ social anxiety or shyness
_____ feeling "different" from others
_____ fear of rejection, abandonment or being alone
_____ fear of failure
_____ fear of criticism, confrontation or anger
_____ oversensitivity (including defensiveness)
_____ excessive feelings of guilt
_____ martyrdom or "victim syndrome"
_____ frequently comparing self to others
_____ unrealistic expectations toward self or others
_____ perfectionism
_____ taking life or self too seriously, difficulty having fun
_____ rigidity, inflexibility or controlling tendencies
_____ chaotic or overflexible tendencies
_____ not being able to take things seriously enough
_____ procrastination or indecisiveness
_____ extreme loyalty to others
_____ people-pleasing or approval-seeking tendencies
_____ non-assertiveness (passivity or passive-aggressiveness)
_____ ignoring or not expressing self and own needs and feelings
_____ caretaking or super-responsibility for others
_____ stereotyping people
_____ aggressiveness or resentment (holding grudges)
_____ jealousy or envy
_____ super-irresponsibility or not keeping agreements
_____ nondisclosure of self (including fear of "being found out")
_____ dishonesty or manipulative tendencies
_____ avoidance of commitments (includes fear of feeling "trapped")
_____ overuse of defense mechanisms (e.g., denial, blame)
_____ other _____

Focusing on developing healthy relationships is an important life skill!

BREAKING DOWN OUR WALLS

I. PURPOSE:

To increase awareness of attitude and behavior patterns that reduce potential for quality relationships.

To identify more constructive ways of relating to others.

II. GENERAL COMMENTS:

It is all too easy to get stuck in the cycle of dysfunctional patterns that we may have learned within our family dynamics. However, it is important to realize that we are not victims of our past and that we can learn more effective ways of relating to others.

III. POSSIBLE ACTIVITIES:

A. 1. Distribute handout and review.

2. Ask the group to share which listed attitudes and behaviors were demonstrated by various family members when they were growing up and/or are present in their current relationships, giving examples. Include discussion on how the different patterns relate to each other, e.g., addicts may be associated with co-dependents, martyrs/victims with aggressors/manipulators.

3. Instruct group to break into pairs and share what healthier relationship qualities they would like to attract and create in their lives.

4. Reconvene as one group and encourage each member to restate his/her partner's response as they understand it, offering feedback as appropriate.

5. Process benefits of this activity.

B. 1. Distribute handout.

2. Ask group which of the listed behaviors and attitudes they exhibit in current relationships.

3. Discuss the payoffs or what they get out of maintaining various unhealthy patterns, e.g., get to justify or excuse to stay stuck, perceiving power or control, escape.

4. Ask what it has cost them and how it will hurt them to continue these patterns, e.g., lowers self-respect, fosters resentments.

5. Instruct the group to state their plan for change; what new attitudes and behaviors they will practice in order to develop healthier relationships, e.g., assertiveness, tolerance, letting go of control.

6. Question group on how they will benefit by acting out these new behavior patterns, e.g., increased self-esteem, recovery, loving relationships.

7. Process benefits of this activity.

Activity handout and facilitator's information submitted by Dotty D. Gardler, M.S., CTRS, Philadelphia, PA.

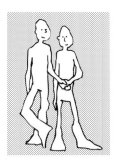

Characteristics of

HEALTHY
RELATIONSHIPS

How many of the following attitudes and behaviors are present in your relationships?

- ☐ communication is open and spontaneous (including listening)
- ☐ rules/boundaries are clear and explicit, yet allows flexibility
- ☐ individuality, freedom and personal identity is enhanced
- ☐ each enjoys doing things for self, as well as for the other
- ☐ play, humor, and having fun together is commonplace
- ☐ each does not attempt to "fix" or control the other
- ☐ acceptance of self and other (for <u>real</u> selves)
- ☐ assertiveness: feelings and needs are expressed
- ☐ humility: able to let go of need to "be right"
- ☐ self-confidence and security in own worth
- ☐ conflict is faced directly and resolved
- ☐ openness to constructive feedback
- ☐ each is trustful of the other
- ☐ balance of giving and receiving
- ☐ negotiations are fair and democratic
- ☐ tolerance: forgiveness of self and other
- ☐ mistakes are accepted and learned from
- ☐ willingness to take risks and be vulnerable
- ☐ other meaningful relationships and interests exist
- ☐ each can enjoy being alone and privacy is respected
- ☐ personal growth, change and exploration is encouraged
- ☐ continuity and consistency is present in the commitment
- ☐ balance of oneness (closeness) and separation from each other
- ☐ responsibility for own behaviors and happiness (not blaming other)
- ☐ _____
- ☐ _____
- ☐ _____

DEVELOPING HEALTHY RELATIONSHIPS IS AN IMPORTANT LIFE SKILL!

Characteristics of
HEALTHY RELATIONSHIPS

I. PURPOSE:

To identify healthier, more constructive, relationship patterns.

II. GENERAL COMMENTS:

When one grows up with and continues dysfunctional relationship patterns, it is a common phenomenon to not know what "normal" is. Therefore, in order for one to make changes, it helps to learn the difference between what are healthy and what are unhealthy ways of relating to others.

III. POSSIBLE ACTIVITIES:

A. 1. Review handout with the group.

   2. Ask group to share which characteristics they already demonstrate in their relationships, giving specific examples. Also, encourage group to give examples or names of group members who have demonstrated these behaviors within the group itself.

   3. Hand out a sheet of blank paper to each participant and instruct them to draw a line down the middle. On one side, tell them to list what healthy relationship attitudes and behaviors that they would like to have in their lives. On the other side, they are to list current negative attitudes and behaviors that they are willing to stop, or let go of, in order to achieve what they want.

   4. Process activity by asking the group to share what they had listed, in addition to what specific plans or actions they will take to make these changes.

B. 1. Review handout with the group.

   2. Introduce concept of role-playing, informing group of the benefits and procedures of this technique.

   3. Explain to the group that various role-play situations have been prepared ahead of time and that each will require successful demonstration of an assigned relationship characteristic (similar to those listed on the handout). Assign or have group members volunteer to act out each of the situations and assigned behaviors. After every role-play, ask participants to share about their experiences.

   4. Encourage feedback from the remainder of the group, e.g., what was done well or what could have been done more effectively and how.

   5. Process benefits of this activity.

Activity handout and facilitator's information submitted by Dotty D. Gardler, M.S., CTRS, Philadelphia, PA.

Keeping Our Commitments

Covenant of _____
                                    (name)

Target Date: _____

A) Three goals I will have accomplished (e.g., related to self,
    relationships, career, or health):
      1. _____
      2. _____
      3. _____

B) Two social supports or groups with which I will be actively
    involved (e.g., individuals, leisure or support groups):
      1. _____
      2. _____

C) One area of unfinished business that I will have taken care of
    (e.g., cleaned-up relationship, made amends):
      1. _____

D) Two constructive coping techniques (e.g., calling a friend,
    setting limits) that I will have successfully used to deal with
    self-sabotaging behavior are:
      1. _____
      2. _____

E) How I will deal with any broken integrity or unkept
    commitments (e.g., self-esteem work, apologies):
      1. _____
      2. _____
      3. _____

Signature: _____
Witness: _____
Date: _____

Keeping Our Commitments

I. PURPOSE:

To improve the quality of personal relationships by identifying and practicing personal commitment-making.

II. GENERAL COMMENTS:

Saying that we plan to do something or change for the better is often easy to say in the moment, but all too easily forgotten, as we continue to stay set in our ways day after day. However, stating our goals to others combined with periodic "reminders" can be a results-producing technique.

III. POSSIBLE ACTIVITIES:

A. 1. Introduce topic of commitment-making. Have group discuss ways in which we self-sabotage our goals and possible coping techniques for dealing with self-sabotage, setbacks, and broken integrity.

2. Distribute handouts and assign the task of completing it as is, or have them write a letter to themselves, using the handout as a guideline. Give the group a target date before they begin, e.g., 2 months from now.

3. Ask the group to share their commitments and encourage feedback.

4. Give an envelope to everyone and instruct them to self-address it and insert their completed exercise.

5. Inform the group that their exercise will be mailed to them before the designated target date as a "wake-up call" for self-evaluation.

6. Process benefits of this activity.

B. 1. Review handout with the group and assign a target date (a date within which group members will still be together).

2. Instruct the group to divide into smaller groups or partners.

3. Ask them to complete the exercise together by verbally stating their commitments.

4. Reassemble the entire group and process their findings and reactions.

5. Give the assignment that everyone is to meet with their partners or small groups at designated or self-appointed times. They should meet for the purpose of increasing individual accountability and integrity, for ongoing feedback, and as a support system for assisting individuals with fulfilling their commitments.

6. Process benefits of this activity.

Activity handout and facilitator's information submitted by Dotty D. Gardler, M.S., CTRS, Philadelphia, PA.

RELATIONSHIPS
AND YOU

List three personal traits you like in others:

1. _____ 2. _____ 3. _____

List three personal traits you dislike in others:

1. _____ 2. _____ 3. _____

Name three positive qualities you bring or could bring to a relationship:

1. _____ 2. _____ 3. _____

Name three personal accomplishments or achievements you'd enjoy sharing with someone:

1. _____ 2. _____ 3. _____

List any self-defeating behaviors you see in yourself:

1. _____ 2. _____ 3. _____

Name persons you like from different backgrounds other than your own:

1. _____ 2. _____ 3. _____

How do you nurture love and friendship?

_____

_____

RELATIONSHIPS AND YOU

I. PURPOSE:

To provide insight into the personal qualities one brings to relationships.

II. GENERAL COMMENTS:

Healthy relationships involve understanding and accepting oneself and others.

III. POSSIBLE ACTIVITIES:

A. 1. Distribute handouts. Encourage group members to fill out their answers and share these with each other.

2. Make a list of positive and negative personal traits seen in others; these lists could be cumulative.

3. Write the name of each group member on a separate piece of paper. Pass these around, asking each person to write something positive about that member. Return to the appropriate individuals and ask them to read their list to the group.

4. Discuss self-defeating behaviors and make a list with group input.

5. Have available pamphlets, articles, audiotapes and videotapes on nurturing love and friendship, e.g., *In Search of Joy* video.

6. Discuss the positive benefits of diversity in relationships.

B. 1. Facilitate discussion of importance of healthy relationships. What do you get from healthy relationships? How do we benefit?

2. Distribute handouts and instruct group members to complete.

3. Share by asking group members to read aloud one statement and their responses.

4. Ask group members to identify which was the easiest and the most difficult. Try to pair group members using a "buddy system" for 3-5 minutes to explore specific questions. Offer the pairs sample questions for mini-discussion, e.g., one group member can ask the other member of the pair, "What hints can you share with me to make this easier?" Reconvene as large group.

5. Process by asking group members to identify one new aspect of themselves and healthy relationships which they've learned by this activity.

Activity handout and facilitator's information submitted by Bettie Michelson, MS, OTR, De Kalb, IL.

BREADWINNER

is not enough in today's world!

Currently in today's society, traditional roles are changing rapidly for both men and women. More and more men are starting to get involved with parenting and household management. Identify by checking off whether you feel COMFORT or DISCOMFORT in the following roles, then check off whether you perceive these roles as being MALE or FEMALE.

I. HOUSEHOLD MANAGER	COMFORT	DISCOMFORT	MALE	FEMALE
Meal preparation	☐	☐	☐	☐
Meal planning	☐	☐	☐	☐
Making shopping list	☐	☐	☐	☐
Grocery shopping	☐	☐	☐	☐
Bathroom cleaning (tub, sink, toilet)	☐	☐	☐	☐
Money management	☐	☐	☐	☐
Entertaining	☐	☐	☐	☐
Holiday / special occasion planning	☐	☐	☐	☐
Dusting	☐	☐	☐	☐
Vacuuming	☐	☐	☐	☐
Washing / waxing floor	☐	☐	☐	☐
Laundry	☐	☐	☐	☐
Dishes	☐	☐	☐	☐
Home repairs	☐	☐	☐	☐
Yard maintenance	☐	☐	☐	☐
Auto maintenance	☐	☐	☐	☐

II. PARENT				
Meal planning	☐	☐	☐	☐
Care of children	☐	☐	☐	☐
Transportation to or from daycare/ preschool	☐	☐	☐	☐
Sex education	☐	☐	☐	☐
Play	☐	☐	☐	☐
Doctor's visits	☐	☐	☐	☐
Toilet training	☐	☐	☐	☐
Illness / medication management	☐	☐	☐	☐
Providing emotional support	☐	☐	☐	☐
Showing affection	☐	☐	☐	☐
Buying clothing for children	☐	☐	☐	☐
Discipline	☐	☐	☐	☐
Talking and listening to your child	☐	☐	☐	☐
Awareness of developmental ages and stages	☐	☐	☐	☐
Selecting daily appropriate clothing	☐	☐	☐	☐
Assisting child with homework	☐	☐	☐	☐

By exploring these new roles, you will find both challenges _and_ rewards!

Men's Changing Roles:

BREADWINNER is not enough in today's world!

I. PURPOSE:

To explore and gain insight into men's new emerging roles.

II. GENERAL COMMENTS:

It has been the rule in our society for a long time that it is a woman's responsibility to take care of the children and home and for the man to be the "breadwinner". Currently in today's society, traditional roles are changing rapidly, both for men and women. More men are starting to get involved with child care and household management.

III. POSSIBLE ACTIVITIES:

A. 1. Distribute handouts.

2. Define men's traditional and non-traditional roles.

3. Instruct group members to complete handout.

4. Discuss with group members the following questions:

a. How do you feel about your rating?

b. What roadblocks can you identify that prevent you from participating in non-traditional roles?

c. What changes would you like to make?

d. What is stopping you from making changes?

e. How will you go about making those changes?

f. How does your upbringing have an influence on your ability to participate in non-traditional roles?

5. Process the group by discussing insights gained from this activity.

B. 1. Distribute handouts.

2. Define men's traditional and non-traditional roles.

3. Role-play family interactions involving non-traditional roles.
Ex: Men role-playing an activity in which they feel discomfort and which they perceive as primarily a female role.
Females role-play an activity in which they feel discomfort and which they perceive as primarily a male role.

4. Encourage discussion of role-play, providing feedback and support.

5. Process benefits of this activity and insights gained from activity.

Activity handout and facilitator's information submitted by Hector L. Merced, OTR/L and Deena Baenen, M.A., COTA/L, Cleveland, OH.

ENVISIONING

FEMALE Role Models

role model: a person who is unusually effective or inspiring in some social role, job, position, etc., and so serves as a model for others.

When learning or practicing the skill of envisioning female role models, look for and choose *specific* qualities, characteristics, and/or accomplishments of a *variety* of women, as empowering images.

Here are 10 examples of the many outstanding qualities, characteristics, and/or accomplishments some females have and 10 females who possess them:

1. **ADVOCATE**
Patty Duke, diagnosed with manic-depressive illness at age 35, speaks publicly, educating people about mental illness.

2. **ARTISTIC**
Leontyne Price, was the first black woman to achieve worldwide status in opera. She is noted for her role in "Aida".

3. **ATHLETIC**
Nadia Comaneci, at age 14, was the first athlete ever to achieve a score of 10 in the Olympics.

4. **COMPASSIONATE**
Mary Ayala, chose to have a baby, in hopes of her having compatible bone marrow for a transplant for other daughter, who was dying of leukemia (and is now free of cancer!).

5. **COURAGEOUS**
Hannah Senesh, in 1944, was court-martialed, then brutally tortured and executed, when caught trying to rescue the Jews from Hungary.

6. **FORERUNNERS IN A "MAN'S WORLD"**
Judith Resnick, was second woman to fly in space, and worked on the remote manipulator system (shuttle's robot arm). She died on a mission in 1986.

7. **LEADERSHIP**
Betty Friedan, in 1966, founded and became president of National Organization for Women (NOW), and is author of "The Feminine Mystique" and "The Fountain of Age".

8. **RESPONSIBLE FOR PUBLIC AWARENESS**
Joan Baez, famous folksinger, who during the '60's was prominent in the civil rights and antiwar movements.

9. **RISK TAKERS**
Kimberly Bergalis, believed to be the first person to contract AIDS from her dentist, spent her years fighting for rights of AIDS victims, before Congress and the USA. She died in 1992.

10. **TRIUMPHANT IN OVERCOMING ODDS**
Ann Jillian, actress and singer, who publicly battled and conquered breast cancer. In 1985 she began a crusade for early detection of cancer.

Complete the following section with names of your role-model images. They can be well-known women, fictional or non-fictional, as well as women you personally know.

1. _____
2. _____
3. _____
4. _____
5. _____

6. _____
7. _____
8. _____
9. _____
10. _____

Make a GOAL to use one positive role-model image for situations you find yourself in each day!

ENVISIONING
FEMALE
Role Models

I. PURPOSE:

To increase self-esteem by recognizing and identifying specific role models to use as positive images.

II. GENERAL COMMENTS:

Traditionally, boys and men are provided with and use a variety of role models with a variety of male characteristics. Girls and women on the other hand, have traditionally been provided with female role models who possessed caretaking, nurturing or giving characteristics. Although these characteristics are admirable and desirable, they are not the only ones that girls/women need to acquire – leadership, courage, etc. – are also valued and needed.

III. POSSIBLE ACTIVITIES:

A. 1. Review material presented above.

   2. List on the chalkboard participants' present female role models, asking what specific characteristics that they have that are admired or liked.

   3. Distribute handouts and read aloud.

   4. Complete the handout by forming triads, asking each group of 3 to identify as many potential role models as they can in 1-3 categories – leadership, courage, etc. After 5 minutes, ask each triad to present their list. Discuss.

   5. Instruct group members to now complete their handouts individually.

   6. Process the group asking each group member to identify one positive role model and the specific characteristic that they will use as a positive image.

B. 1. Discuss concept of role models and their potentially positive influences on individuals' choices and behaviors.

   2. Relate information from general comments section about traditional female role models. Distribute handouts, complete and discuss responses.

   3. Brainstorm on chalkboard a list of 10 or more professions that women are involved in, e.g., physician, businesswoman, secretary, educator, etc.

   4. Elicit from group members several women in each profession who they feel are positive role models (women they know directly or indirectly).

   5. Discuss the impact these women have had on their lives, or can have.

   6. Process benefits of this activity and conclude by setting goals to use specific positive female role models as motivators to make personal change.

ENVISIONING
MALE Role Models

role model: a person who is unusually effective or inspiring in some social role, job, position, etc., and so serves as a model for others.

When learning or practicing the skill of envisioning male role models, look for and choose *specific* qualities, characteristics, and/or accomplishments of a *variety* of men, as empowering images.

Here are 10 examples of the many outstanding qualities, characteristics, and/or accomplishments some males have and 10 males who possess them:

1. **ACTOR/ACTIVIST** — *Robert Redford*, starred in many films including "The Way We Were", and "The Sting". He speaks out and promotes the rights of Native Americans and works diligently in the environmental movement.

2. **ARTISTIC** — *Kahlil Gibran*, early 20th century poet and artist. The Prophet is well-known world-wide and remains an eloquent testimony of mankind's highest aspirations. He was a vocal spokesperson for minority and women's rights.

3. **COOL-HEADEDNESS** — *Joe Montana*, arguably the best quarterback who has ever played football. One of the leaders in the NFL of fourth quarter comebacks. With Joe in the huddle, no situation ever seemed insurmountable.

4. **CULTURAL** — *Robert Bly*, a National Book Award winner. Iron John was on the New York Times best-seller list for a year. His love of poetry led him to translate many non-American poems into English, enriching the lives of many people.

5. **DIPLOMAT OF GOOD WILL** — *Ervin "Magic" Johnson*, NBA superstar. Despite the fame and the contraction of AIDS, he still works tirelessly and speaks out vigorously on social issues that affect us all.

6. **INSPIRATIONAL ORATOR** — *Dr. Martin Luther King, Jr.*, Nobel laureate. Acknowledged leader of the 1960's Civil Rights Movement. One of the most eloquent and passionate speakers of any era.

7. **LEADERSHIP** — *Jean-Luc Picard*, the fictional captain of the "Starship Enterprise". A skilled diplomat, slow to anger, exercises good judgement and is judicious in his use of force. He is sensitive to his officers' needs.

8. **LOVE OF NATURE** — *John Muir*, naturalist writer. With passion and love for America's wilderness, he helped to push forward an environmental agenda to preserve our greatest natural resources. Yosemite National Park and others exist today largely due to his efforts.

9. **STRENGTH OF CONVICTION** — *Mahatma Ghandi*, the central figure of India's independence movement. Staunch opponent of racism and religious intolerance. Firm believer of non-violent protest.

10. **WISDOM** — *Michael Meade*, storyteller, scholar of mythology, literature, and ritual in traditional cultures. Meade brings to life ancient stories that reveal places where the soul has hidden from our modern culture.

Complete the following section with names of your role-model images. They can be well-known men, fictional or non-fictional, as well as men you personally know.

1. _____
2. _____
3. _____
4. _____
5. _____

6. _____
7. _____
8. _____
9. _____
10. _____

Make a GOAL to use one positive role-model image for situations you find yourself in each day!

ENVISIONING
MALE
Role Models

I.   PURPOSE:

To increase self-esteem by recognizing and identifying specific role models to use as positive images.

II.   GENERAL COMMENTS:

Historically in our culture the number of role models that men and boys have had to look up to were severely limited. The ones that were presented, usually by Hollywood, were cut out of the same mold, e.g., John Wayne, Humphrey Bogart, Sylvester Stallone, etc. The qualities of fearlessness, leadership and ruggedness, while important, are not the only ones men and boys need to acquire. Sensitivity, emotional availability and kindness are also needed and important.

III.   POSSIBLE ACTIVITIES:

A. 1. Review material presented above.

2. List on the chalkboard participants' present male role models, asking what specific characteristics they have that are admired or liked.

3. Distribute handouts and read aloud.

4. Complete the handout by forming triads, asking each group of 3 to identify as many potential role models as they can in 1-3 categories – kindness, sensitivity, etc. After 5 minutes, ask each triad to present their list. Discuss.

5. Instruct group members to now complete their handouts individually.

6. Process the group, asking each group member to identify one positive role model and the specific characteristic that they will use as a positive image.

B. 1. Discuss concept of role models and their potentially positive influences on individuals' choices and behaviors.

2. Relate information from general comments section about traditional male role models. Distribute handouts, complete and discuss responses.

3. Brainstorm on chalkboard a list of 10 or more professions that men are involved in, e.g., physician, businessman, secretary, educator, etc.

4. Elicit from group members several men in each profession who they feel are positive role models (men they know directly or indirectly).

5. Discuss the impact these men have had on their lives, or can have.

6. Process benefits of this activity and conclude by setting goals to use specific positive male role models as motivators to make personal change.

Activity handout and facilitator's information adapted by Siri-Dya S. Khalsa, M.Ed., Hudson, OH.

Juggling *vs.* Balancing

Women today often have an overwhelming list of responsibilities. Even though a large number of women are now also employed *outside* of the home, they have not given up their traditional *full-time* responsibilities *inside* the home. For these women, it has become more difficult to maintain a BALANCE in their lives. Day after day, they JUGGLE these added responsibilities at work *and* in the home, often becoming distressed and dissatisfied with many or all of their life roles.

Below is a typical list of responsibilities and/or activities with which women may be involved. Read and check off those that apply to you, then refer to the balance basics for helpful ideas!

- ☐ Meal preparation
- ☐ Menu planning
- ☐ Dishes
- ☐ Housecleaning
- ☐ Laundry
- ☐ Grocery shopping
- ☐ Yard work
- ☐ Home maintenance
- ☐ Pet care
- ☐ Decorating
- ☐ Entertaining
- ☐ Bills
- ☐ Care of children
- ☐ Care of parents
- ☐ Care of spouse
- ☐ Care of others

- ☐ Necessity shopping
- ☐ Plant care
- ☐ Car maintenance
- ☐ Budgeting
- ☐ Parent-Teacher meetings
- ☐ Car-pooling
- ☐ Calendar scheduling
- ☐ Doctor appts. - self/kids
- ☐ 1:1 with family members
- ☐ Taxes
- ☐ Necessity phone calling
- ☐ Trash collection / recycling
- ☐ Time with friends
- ☐ Classes
- ☐ Homework / assignments
- ☐ Seminars for career / job

- ☐ Career / job tasks at work
- ☐ Career / job tasks at home
- ☐ Commute time
- ☐ Exercise / fitness
- ☐ Work / business travel
- ☐ Pleasure travel
- ☐ Family outings
- ☐ Special events planning
- ☐ Grooming
- ☐ Bathing
- ☐ Dressing
- ☐ Eating
- ☐ Sleeping
- ☐ Volunteer work
- ☐ Church / synagogue
- ☐ Community involvement

- ☐ Charity activities
- ☐ Sports activities
- ☐ Television
- ☐ Music
- ☐ Reading
- ☐ Cultural arts
- ☐ Hobbies
- ☐ Computer work / play
- ☐ Singing
- ☐ Dancing
- ☐ Movies
- ☐ Alone time
- ☐ _____
- ☐ _____
- ☐ _____

WOW! What a list! Chances are you checked off a lot of these and are *now* feeling very overwhelmed . . . "How can I *ever* do all of this?" . . . you may ask.

Now read the following "BALANCE BASICS" for survival tips and lifestyle changes you can make to help you cope on a day-to-day basis.

- ☺ **Prioritize** – you need to get back in touch with what is truly necessary and important to you. Remember, it's OK to say "no" when you need to.
- ☺ **Re-establish your value system** – many decisions about how to spend your time will be guided by your values.
- ☺ **Set daily/weekly/monthly goals** – to keep yourself focused and on track! Remember to write them down and post them in a visible place.
- ☺ **Delegate whenever possible** – involve family members, friends, co-workers, etc. in jobs / activities that do not exclusively need to be done by you.
- ☺ **Organize your work and home environments** – you will spend less time looking for things and more quality time doing things!
- ☺ **Change your expectations about the number of tasks you can cram into one day** – remember balance involves allowing time daily for rest & relaxation too!
- ☺ **Take a mental inventory of all the reasons why you work outside of the home** – try to view your decision to work as a "choice".
- ☺ **Keep communication lines open** – with kids, spouse / significant other, boss, co-workers – your feelings, needs and wants can be known and respected!
- ☺ **Maintain a positive mental attitude and sense of humor and flexibility** – most difficult situations can be worked through if you keep your wits about you!
- ☺ **Plan for leisure/play time, alone and with others** – it won't just happen on its own with a schedule this busy! – the same for exercise!
- ☺ **Find ways to eat nutritiously, yet cut back on grocery shopping and meal preparation time** – hire someone to help! Involve older children too!
- ☺ **Manage laundry** – find a pick-up and delivery service / hire help / do 1 or 2 loads a day / each family member does own laundry / set a routine!
- ☺ **Make use of "waiting-in-line, waiting room, and traffic jam time"** – keep small tasks with you to do when these situations arise!
- ☺ **Use one central calendar** – for meal planning, bills, appointments, events, schedules, responsibilities – an excellent way to organize all household goings-on.
- ☺ **Remember to respect yourself** – make healthy choices and changes as needed to keep you in balance day after day. Pace yourself. Enjoy life!
- ☺ _____

Juggling *vs.* Balancing

I. PURPOSE:

To increase role satisfaction of women by learning to achieve life balance.

To identify specific lifestyle changes that women can make to bring about this balance.

II. GENERAL COMMENTS:

Many women are caught in the "superwoman syndrome" trap – trying to *do it all* – and eventually feeling like doing *nothing* because of burnout. They continually *juggle* an overwhelming list of responsibilities and activities, functioning *out-of-balance* much of the time. This ongoing struggle usually leads to stress, frustration, fatigue and dissatisfaction with many or all life roles.

III. POSSIBLE ACTIVITIES:

A. 1. Distribute handouts to all group members, first reviewing concept of BALANCE as opposed to JUGGLING.

    2. Instruct group members to complete handout by checking off those responsibilities/activities they currently are juggling. Then, ask them to mark the BALANCE BASICS that they are willing to put into action to improve role satisfaction.

    3. Allow 15-20 minutes for completion and then reconvene as a large group for discussion of responses.

    4. Process group by asking group members to (1) identify three BALANCE BASICS they plan to use and (2) identify benefits of this activity.

B. 1. Discuss with group the concept of BALANCE as opposed to JUGGLING.

    2. Brainstorm on chalkboard a list of responsibilities/activities that group members have at home and work.

    3. Emphasize that sometimes women need to learn more effective time management and assertive skills to achieve balance, whereas other times they actually need to reduce or change life roles.

    4. Prior to group, prepare 15 index cards with one BALANCE BASIC written on each. Taking turns, ask group members to randomly choose a card from the deck and respond by (1) stating whether they currently use this tip; (2) whether they plan to use it in the future to assist with balance; and/or (3) how they plan to implement it.

    5. Continue until all BALANCE BASICS have been discussed.

    6. Distribute handouts to all group members and instruct all to complete as a means of personalizing this activity.

    7. Process benefits of achieving balance in life roles and responsibilities.

Awareness Journal

	SITUATION DATE TIME	PHYSICAL SURROUNDINGS	BODY'S PHYSICAL REACTIONS	BEHAVIORS	EMOTIONS	INNER VOICE	VALUES
What happened?							
What can I do next time?	☐ No change ☐ Change:	☐ No change ☐ Change:	☐ No change ☐ Change:	☐ No change ☐ Change:	☐ No change ☐ Change:	☐ No change ☐ Change:	☐ No change ☐ Change:

Awareness Journal

I. PURPOSE:

To increase awareness and insight into how physical surroundings, the body's physical reactions, behaviors, emotions, inner voice and values affect or influence specific situations.

II. GENERAL COMMENTS:

So many factors affect each situation or interaction that presents itself. Unless we "freeze the moment" to analyze them, we might lose valuable information. At times, certain factors influence a situation more than others, but all are worth evaluating.

III. POSSIBLE ACTIVITIES:

A. 1. Present the handout, defining each of the factors as follows:

   a. physical surroundings – where were you? lighting? noises? smells? sights? tastes?

   b. body's physical reactions – what did your body do? breathing? temperature? sweat? become more active? less active? pain or aches anywhere?

   c. behaviors – what did you do?

   d. emotions – how did you feel? anxious? sad? happy? excited? resentful? regretful?

   e. inner voice – what were your self-thoughts?

   f. values – what beliefs, perceptions, values affected you? What "guided" your action?

   2. Illustrate the concept on a chalkboard or flip chart – using a group member's example. First, fill in the "what happened" line. Then, re-work the example in the next line with increased awareness. What factors can be changed? What factors can't or don't need to be changed? Discuss with group members that each factor is important and can potentially affect all other components!

   3. Ask group members to complete using a recent situation.

   4. Share as able.

   5. Give a 1-week assignment to each group member using 7 sheets, stapled together.

   6. Process by asking thought-provoking questions such as: Which factors seem to have valuable information? Which factors have the highest potential for change?

B. 1. Discuss concept of journal writing and its importance, encouraging group members to share their experience as appropriate.

   2. Distribute handouts and explain all categories as in A.1. Ask group members to complete. Offer following example or one of your own:

	SITUATION DATE TIME	PHYSICAL SURROUNDINGS	BODY'S PHYSICAL REACTIONS	BEHAVIORS	EMOTIONS	INNER VOICE	VALUES
What happened?	Talking with previous supervisor of a recent past job. 11-9 2:00 p.m.	My home. Talking on telephone. Relaxing with a T.V. program in back-ground.	Tired. Butterflies in stomach. Tense.	"Over-explained" my purpose in making call. Defensive when questioned. Controlling conversation.	Irritable. Nervous. Angry. Impatient.	"I feel demeaned when asked so many questions." "I want her to agree with my opinion." "I can't wait to end this conversation."	Good Intensions. Hard work. Dedication. Commitment. Creativity. Motivation.
What can I do next time?	☑ No change ☐ Change:	☑ No change ☐ Change:	☐ No change ☑ Change: Deep breathing to relax prior to and during conversation (if needed).	☐ No change ☑ Change: More assertive approach. State purpose in clear, concise manner. Respond to questions openly.	☐ No change ☑ Change: Determined. Confident. Enthusiastic. Calm.	☐ No change ☑ Change: "I know my request is reasonable and in both of our best interests." "I can be assertive with her even though she is not with me."	☑ No change ☐ Change:

   3. Encourage group members to form groups of three for discussion of responses.

   4. Reconvene as large group and conclude by asking group members to state 1 positive thing they have learned from this activity.

ME, MY SELF-AWARENESS, AND I

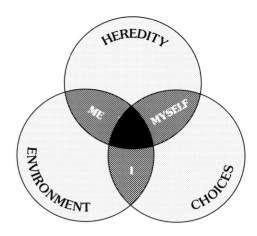

Please complete with as many details as you can:

HEREDITY

How I was made:
(physical characteristics, traits, tendencies)

_____

_____

_____

_____

\+

ENVIRONMENT

When I grew up:
Where I grew up:
How I grew up:
What I learned:
(values)

_____

_____

_____

_____

\+

MY CHOICES

Positive and negative choices that I make:

_____

_____

_____

_____

_____

= ME

ME, MY SELF-AWARENESS, AND I

I. PURPOSE:

To increase self-awareness by recognizing it is not only heredity and / or environment that make a person – but also the choices that a person makes in his / her life.

II. GENERAL COMMENTS:

This presents a twist to the age-old argument of heredity vs. environment. At times, it is not within our immediate power to change either one. The idea that choices influence an individual, offers a sense of hope and self-empowerment, because individuals <u>do</u> have control of their choices.

III. POSSIBLE ACTIVITIES:

A. 1. Distribute handouts, discussing the topic and benefits of greater self-awareness.

2. Brainstorm on chalkboard group members' responses to possible answers for:
   <u>HEREDITY-</u>
   <u>How I was made (physical characteristics, traits, tendencies):</u> physical qualities, assets, limitations, handicaps, etc.

   <u>ENVIRONMENT-</u>
   <u>When I grew up:</u> various time periods (60's, wars, depression, etc.)
   <u>Where I grew up:</u> details of house, urban or rural, city, country, etc.
   <u>How I grew up:</u> socioeconomic status, familial relationships, etc.
   <u>What I learned (values):</u> education, work, positive and negative life experiences, etc.

   <u>MY CHOICES-</u>
   <u>Positive and negative choices that I make:</u> Coping strategies, assertive skills, social relationships, limit setting, arguing, use of substances, revengeful behavior, etc.

3. Distribute index cards and ask each member to fill out 3 cards.

   Card #1 - How I was made.
   Card #2 - When / Where / How I grew up / What I learned.
   Card #3 - Positive and negative choices.

   Be sure each card is numbered correctly.

4. Shuffle #1's together, then #2's and #3's. Pass out mixed cards – each member receiving a "new" #1, #2, and #3 card.

5. Ask members to share their cards and identify how it might feel to be this "fictional" person. What would they choose to do if they were in this situation?

6. Instruct all group members to now complete their handouts with their own responses.

7. Discuss briefly as a group and process benefits of this activity.

B. 1. Distribute handouts to all group members and discuss.

2. Ask group members to complete the handout, writing their first name in the "ME" section.

3. Cut handouts horizontally into 4 sections, i.e., heredity, environment, my choices, and ME, and mix all members' papers on a large table.

4. Ask members to gather around a large table and choose another member's name.

5. Encourage each member to try and piece the papers back together correctly and return them to their owners!

6. Instruct group to share responses.

7. Process benefits of this activity.

Activity handout and facilitator's information submitted by Rebecca Cook, OTR, Petersburg, MI.

REACTION 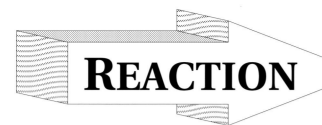 PATTERNS

We can learn a great deal about ourselves by taking a look at our usual REACTION in a given situation. Oftentimes, we will see PATTERNS in our behavior. This information offers us increased self-awareness, which can be helpful in changing our *future* reactions in these situations as needed.

Think about the following situations and – to the best of your ability – write, draw, or symbolize how you *usually* or *most often* tend to react:

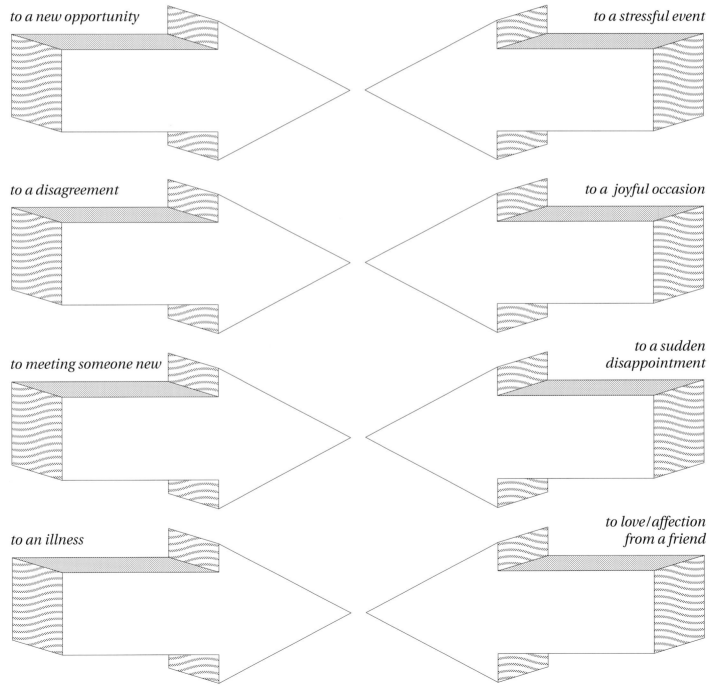

to a new opportunity

to a stressful event

to a disagreement

to a joyful occasion

to meeting someone new

to a sudden disappointment

to an illness

to love/affection from a friend

REACTION PATTERNS

I. PURPOSE:

To increase self-awareness regarding reactions to various situations.

To identify patterns of behavior that may need to be changed.

II. GENERAL COMMENTS:

Although human behavior is not *always* consistent, it may often be fairly predictable through recognizing reaction patterns over a period of time. With this knowledge, individuals can identify specific behaviors that need to be changed to increase healthy living.

III. POSSIBLE ACTIVITIES:

A. 1. Distribute handouts to all group members and review top portion of handout together.

   2. Instruct group members to complete handout, using a variety of pencils, pens, colored markers, crayons, etc. They can write words, draw pictures, or symbolize their typical reactions in these particular situations, or the facilitator can offer alternate situations.

   3. Allow 15-20 minutes for completion and then share as a group.

   4. Process benefits of identifying reaction patterns and changing certain behaviors.

B. 1. Distribute handouts to all group members and review top portion of handout together.

   2. Ask group members to write in their typical reactions to the listed situations.

   3. Review all group members' handouts as a group, encouraging feedback from others.

   4. Collect all handouts and redistribute so that each member gets another member's handout.

   5. Taking turns, ask group members to choose one situation and reaction from the handout they are holding, that they think needs to be role-played.

   6. Proceed with one role-play per group member until all have participated.

   7. Facilitate supportive ideas from others throughout role-plays.

   8. Process group by asking members what they learned when watching one of their reaction patterns role-played by someone else.

Stamp Out the Stigma

of Mental Illness by Eliminating Labels!

The newspapers, television, movies, advertisements, etc., use labels which perpetuate the stigma (negative attitudes) of mental illness. Many of us are guilty of using those same words in our conversations with our co-workers, friends, relatives, etc.

Which of these words or phrases do you use when describing someone whose behavior is different?

_____ SCHIZO	_____ CRAZY	_____ NUTS
_____ OUT OF IT	_____ WACKO	_____ SICKO
_____ SCREWBALL	_____ BONKERS	_____ BATTY
_____ LOST ONE'S MIND	_____ OFF THEIR ROCKER	_____ MENTAL CASE

_____ _____   _____ _____   _____ _____
_____ _____   _____ _____   _____ _____
_____ _____   _____ _____   _____ _____
_____ _____   _____ _____   _____ _____

Can you think of some other words or phrases that could replace these labels?

1. *upset* _____   2. *different* _____   3. *creative* _____
4. _____   5. _____   6. _____
7. _____   8. _____   9. _____

Stigma comes from ignorance and fear!

People often have a hard time grasping anything they can't understand or predict. Let's ALL help to create awareness and sensitivity toward mental illness by avoiding these stigmatizing words and phrases.

Stamp Out The Stigma

I. PURPOSE:

To increase self-awareness by learning about the stigma of mental illness.

To empower individuals by developing and promoting an awareness that the general public, media, and consumers (recipients of mental health services) have the power to perpetuate or stamp out the stigma of mental illness.

II. GENERAL COMMENTS:

Stigma is a narrow set of negative beliefs – continually reinforced by the media, the mental health system, and others – that damages a large, diverse group of individuals. As a basis for discrimination, exclusion, and differential treatment, stigma greatly reduces the ability of people diagnosed and treated for psychiatric disabilities to live, work, and recover in the community.

(definition of "stigma" from the National Stigma Clearinghouse, 275 Seventh Avenue, 16th floor, New York, NY 10001)

Stigmatization and labels about mental illness prevent many people from getting support and proper treatment.

III. POSSIBLE ACTIVITIES:

A. 1. Discuss concept as stated in General Comments.

2. Distribute handouts.

3. Instruct group members to follow directions as outlined on front of handout. Use this additional list for other stigmatizing words or terms.

bats in the belfry	daffy	loose screws	psycho
batty	deviant	lunatic	spaced-out
berserk	fool	mad-man	stark raving mad
booby-hatch	funny farm	nutty	touched
brain-fried	insane asylum	off-the-wall	unbalanced
buggy	loony-bin	out-of-your-mind	wacky
crazed	loose marbles	possessed	weird

4. List on chalkboard words and phrases to replace labels.

5. Facilitate discussion of how society benefits from contributing members who possess words and phrases listed on the chalkboard, e.g., Ernest Hemingway, writer; Patty Duke, actress; Vivien Leigh, actress; Winston Churchill, statesmen, etc. (refer to People With Mental Illness Enrich our Lives poster and accompanying handout for more names, available from Wellness Reproductions Inc., 1/800/669-9208).

6. Process benefits of this activity.

B. 1. Prepare card game with one stigmatizing word/term on each index card.

2. Discuss concept as stated in General Comments.

3. a. Taking turns, ask group members to choose one card and describe how they would feel being called this word/term or described in this way; and,

b. identify how they would prefer to be described.

4. Continue until all group members have had one turn in choosing a card.

5. Distribute handouts, instructing group members to complete, as stated on front of handout.

6. Discuss implications of using stigmatizing words/terms, and individual responsibility in stamping out stigma.

7. Process benefits of this activity.

Women & Risk Taking

As part of personal growth, many women need to work on their risk-taking skills and become more proficient at risk taking. Too often, we focus on the process it'll take to get us there, and not the reward or outcome when we <u>do</u> get there. Try to first imagine, and then write out, the outcome of possible situations without focusing on the efforts that it might take to get there. Can you see the forest through the trees?

	SITUATION		OUTCOME
EXAMPLE	entering a new, intimate relationship	1	love, affection, friendship
		2	security
		3	excitement, opportunities
EXAMPLE	making an important purchase, e.g., home, car, professional wardrobe, etc.	1	convenience
		2	stability
		3	professional status
1		1	
		2	
		3	
2		1	
		2	
		3	
3		1	
		2	
		3	
4		1	
		2	
		3	

USE THIS OUTCOME-ORIENTED APPROACH NEXT TIME YOU CONSIDER A RISK!

Women & Risk Taking

I. PURPOSE:

To increase risk-taking activities in women by focusing on "outcome" rather than "process".

II. GENERAL COMMENTS:

Although women have come far in the risk-taking arena, there is still work to be done. By focusing on "WHAT WE WANT" instead of "BUT THIS IS WHAT IT WILL TAKE", women can increase their risk- taking profile.

III. POSSIBLE ACTIVITIES:

A. 1. Distribute handouts, first reading top and then discussing given examples.

2. Ask for some real-life examples and write the situations on the chalkboard.

3. Choose one to illustrate for the group, including at least 3 outcomes.

4. Instruct individuals to complete with their own personal examples.

5. Process by asking group members to summarize the group and what they've experienced or learned.

B. 1. Prior to group, prepare a deck of cards consisting of 1-2 dozen different risk-taking situations women may encounter.

2. Distribute handouts to all group members.

3. Introduce topic of risk taking to group by reviewing top of handout and getting members' input.

4. Encourage each member to choose 1-2 cards from the deck, depending on group size.

5. Taking turns, ask each member to read aloud her situation on the card and identify potential outcomes of taking this risk – without discussing the method, path, or process involved.

6. After practicing this method of evaluating risks, ask group members to complete bottom portion of handout on their own.

7. Discuss members' responses as a large group, encouraging support and feedback among members.

8. Process benefits of focusing on outcomes of risk-taking situations, rather than the processes involved.

Write Your Own Progress Note:

DATE	PROGRESS NOTES

Write Your Own Progress Note

I. PURPOSE:

To provide an opportunity to share one's own perception of progress with others.

To receive support and feedback.

II. GENERAL COMMENTS:

Patients or clients frequently feel as if much of their treatment happens around them. This exercise provides an opportunity to assume some control and to share perceptions of treatment and progress.

III. POSSIBLE ACTIVITIES:

A. 1. Distribute handouts.

2. Instruct group members to complete handout, writing a narrative in regard to current status/presentation. Suggest that the narrative be written in the first person, e.g., "I have been attending and participating in all groups".

3. Provide time for each participant to share his/her progress note.

4. Process by asking group members to describe benefits of this activity.

B. 1. Acknowledge that the members of the patient's treatment team regularly (daily or weekly) write notes on the patient as guided by their own perceptions.

2. Brainstorm with the group, identifying and listing on a chalkboard, those elements that are to be included in the progress note. This list may include, but is not limited to:

INTERPERSONAL SKILLS: – cooperation, sociability, self-assertion.
TASK SKILLS: – concentration, attention span, ability to problem solve, following directions, interest in activities.
GENERAL BEHAVIOR: – predominant mood, appearance, responsibility, punctuality.

3. Using the categories as outlined on the board, instruct group members to each write a progress note for him/herself, including agreed-upon criteria (EXAMPLE: sociability, concentration, mood and responsibility). Encourage group members to finish narrative with a statement about what they have been working on (goals) and what they hope to do now (plan).

4. Provide an opportunity for each individual to share his/her perceptions.

Activity handout and facilitator's information submitted by Maggie Moriarty, M. Ed., COTA/L, Hartford, CT.

THE INTERNAL / EXTERNAL MAN

Do you find yourself thinking along this line?. . . "Other men are okay, they are what men are <u>supposed</u> to be. I'm the <u>only</u> one who doesn't measure up. I'm the <u>only</u> one who feels hurt and/or frightened. Other men can "handle it" and I can't because I still feel it. I must not let others, especially other men, see this!"
Think of it this way:

You have a special sign inside that says WHO YOU (the internal man) REALLY ARE AND WHAT YOU FEEL, e.g.,

PLEASE LOVE ME AND ACCEPT ME AS I REALLY AM. SOMETIMES I FEEL. . .

In the sign below, write what your internal sign says:

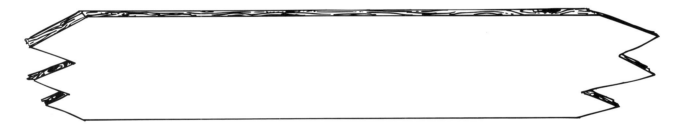

Imagine now the sign that you let others see, that says WHAT YOU (the external man) BELIEVE YOU "SHOULD BE", e.g.,

SEE HOW STRONG, POWERFUL AND SURE OF MYSELF I AM ALL THE TIME. I DON'T NEED. . .

In the sign below, write what your external sign says:

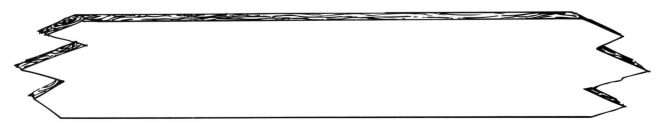

THE INTERNAL / EXTERNAL MAN

I. PURPOSE:

To increase self-esteem by assisting men in identifying, sharing, and accepting their feelings and vulnerable aspects of themselves.

II. GENERAL COMMENTS:

The INTERNAL MAN is defined as "who one really *is* and what one really *feels*" as compared to the EXTERNAL MAN "what one believes one *should be*". Defenses are often used to protect ourselves. Being aware and accepting of the "soft-side" and/or vulnerable aspects of ourselves, allows us to be more true to who we really are and to enhance our self-esteem. It is empowering to recognize that we judge how we FEEL INSIDE against HOW OTHERS APPEAR OUTSIDE. A discussion of this might elicit similar feelings, <u>also</u> enhancing self-esteem.

III. POSSIBLE ACTIVITIES:

A. 1. Distribute handouts and explain concept.

2. Elaborate by offering examples of INTERNAL MAN – "Sometimes, I feel unsure of myself, hurt, and/or frightened. I need you!" and EXTERNAL MAN – "I don't need you or anyone. Don't 'mess' with me. Pay attention to me."

3. Encourage group members to develop their internal and external signs.

4. Have each group member share their internal sign and their external sign. (This will need to be a small group of 6-10 or divide a large group into groups with no more than 6 members.)

5. Encourage group members to give each other feedback related to the accuracy of their signs.

6. Discuss why they think they need external signs and if they need them with everyone and everywhere, or only with certain people and in certain places.

7. Process benefits of activity.

B. 1. Provide each group member with a blank 8½" x 11" piece of paper folded in half.

2. Explain the concept of the external and internal signs.

3. Have each develop their signs on the sheet provided so that the external sign can be read when folded down over the internal sign.

4. Have the group divide into dyads or triads and share their signs.

5. Return to larger groups and process benefits of this activity.

Activity handout and facilitator's information adapted from submission by Sue Bell-Milby, RNC, Wichita, KS.

SELF ESTEEM CROSSWORD PUZZLE

Are you puzzled
... by the importance of self-esteem?
... by it's meaning?
... by the way it enters into everyday conversations?
Try this puzzle... every answer relates to self-esteem.
Have fun while learning these self-esteem terms!

ACROSS

1. confidence and satisfaction in oneself
4. to regard highly; esteem
7. a time for nurturance through activities that are completed without rush or haste
8. strategies, techniques, and tools to manage or balance day-to-day situations or challenges
11. personal development
12. distinguishing quality or characteristic
13. a learned communication style that is honest and direct
15. an aim, an objective, or an intention
16. freedom from influence, control or determination of another or others
19. a behavior that allows one to deal with or attempt to overcome problems, challenges, stressors, and difficult situations
20. to take care of and be good to oneself
21. one's value as a person, as perceived by oneself

DOWN

2. ability to give up resentment or desire to punish, or stop being angry
3. a balance of adequate coping skills, time-effectiveness, and self-control
5. a positive, powerful self-statement concerning the ways in which one desires to think, feel, and/or believe
6. the state of being healthy emotionally, physically, socially, and spiritually
9. awareness of oneself as an individual, and as a worthwhile person
10. moral strength; integrity
14. one's conception of one's own physical self
17. to feel or show honor or esteem
18. pride and self-respect

AFFIRMATION
ASSERTIVE
BODY IMAGE
CHARACTER
COPING
DIGNITY
FORGIVE

GOAL
GROWTH
INDEPENDENCE
LEISURE
LIFE-SKILLS
MANAGEMENT
NURTURE

RESPECT
SELF-CONFIDENT
SELF-ESTEEM
SELF-WORTH
TRAIT
VALUE
WELL-BEING

SELF-ESTEEM CROSSWORD PUZZLE

I. PURPOSE:

To increase self-esteem awareness by becoming knowledgeable of common self-esteem terms and their meanings.

II. GENERAL COMMENTS:

Crossword puzzles are a fun, non-threatening activity. Included are 21 commonly-used terms and brief definitions related to self-esteem.

III. POSSIBLE ACTIVITIES:

A. 1. Distribute handouts.

2. Give group members 10-15 minutes to complete. If group members are able to guess words independently, ask them to cover bottom portion by folding it over.

3. Ask a group member to read "1-Across" definition and his/her answer. Check with below answer key to see if it was a correct response. Continue with rest of puzzle in same way.

ANSWER KEY:

Across	Down
1. self-esteem	2. forgive
4. value	3. management
7. leisure	5. affirmation
8. life-skills	6. well-being
11. growth	9. self-confident
12. trait	10. character
13. assertion	14. body-image
15. goal	17. respect
16. independence	18. dignity
19. coping	
20. nurture	
21. self-worth	

4. Encourage discussion of words with interesting, thought-provoking questions, e.g.,

DIGNITY – Which famous people or characters do we think of when we hear this word?

INDEPENDENCE – How does independence relate to self-esteem?

TRAIT – Describe those traits that come to mind when you think of a person with high self-esteem.

5. Process group and ask each member to identify one word that they can give further thought to in relation to their own self-esteem.

B. 1. Facilitate general discussion of self-esteem to clarify meaning.

2. Brainstorm on chalkboard a list of words often associated with self-esteem.

3. Distribute handouts.

4. Draw group members' attention to word list at bottom of handout to see how many of the 21 words they had identified.

5. Encourage group members to individually complete the crossword, which will emphasize the definitions of these 21 words listed.

6. Discuss as a group to verify answers.

7. Process benefits of understanding self-esteem terms.

REPEATING QUESTIONS

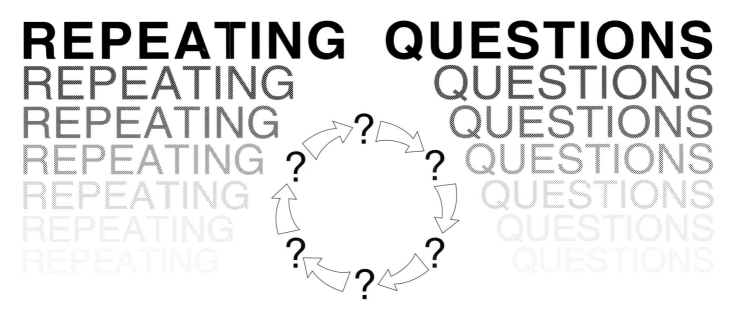

REPEATING QUESTIONS
REPEATING QUESTIONS
REPEATING QUESTIONS
REPEATING QUESTIONS
REPEATING QUESTIONS
REPEATING

REPEATING QUESTIONS explores layers of ourselves and allows us to meet others.

DIRECTIONS:

STEP ONE: A group member volunteers to start.

STEP TWO: He/she turns to the group member on his/her left, says the person's name, and asks one question.

STEP THREE: The person on the left answers and is thanked by the questioner.

STEP FOUR: The person who answered, thanks the questioner. Then, the person who answered, asks the <u>same</u> question to the person on his/her left.

The group proceeds until all people answer the same question, and then another question is asked and the process repeats itself.

---

1. WHAT ARE YOU FEELING RIGHT NOW?

2. WHAT IS SOMETHING YOU ARE AFRAID OF?

3. TELL ME, WHAT DO YOU PRETEND OR IMAGINE?

4. IF THERE IS ONE CHANGE YOU CAN MAKE IN YOUR LIFE, WHAT WOULD IT BE?

5. WHEN DO YOU FEEL "WEAK" OR VULNERABLE?

6. TELL ME SOMETHING YOU LONG FOR OR REALLY WANT?

7. WHAT DO OTHERS HAVE, THAT YOU WANT?

8. IN WHAT WAYS ARE YOU SELF-CRITICAL?

REPEATING QUESTIONS

I. PURPOSE:

To increase social skills by asking questions, listening, and sharing.

II. GENERAL COMMENTS:

REPEATING QUESTIONS teaches the value of open-ended questions, the importance of listening, and how social relationships rely on sharing.

III. POSSIBLE ACTIVITIES:

A. 1. Distribute handouts. Assemble group members in a circle with no tables between them.

2. Engage in the activity as stated on front of handout.

3. Process the group by discussing the following . . .

   - What is the value of questions in social situations?

   - What did you notice about your listening style or the listening style of others?

   - Were there any "stories" told? If yes, what is their value?

   - Did the intensity in the room change from when people first walked into the room, to when the group ended? How?

   - How does sharing affect social relationships?

   - What can group members say that they've learned from this experience?

B. 1. Distribute handouts. Ask group members to form small groups of 3, sitting in a circle with no tables between them.

2. Discuss activity as stated on front of handout, emphasizing basic social skills of asking questions, listening, and sharing. Encourage everyone to be aware of body language during interactions.

3. Instruct small groups to engage in activity for 15 minutes.

4. Reconvene as a large group and continue activity for additional 15 minutes.

5. Discuss with group members any differences they noticed in responses in the small groups vs. the large group, i.e., level of disclosure, eye contact, voice volume/intensity, length of response, etc.

6. Process benefits of practicing basic social skills in both sizes of group.

7. Give homework assignment to practice appropriate questioning, listening, and sharing on 1:1 basis with 3-4 significant people during the next week.

Activity handout and facilitator's information adapted from submission by Siri-Dya S. Khalsa, M.Ed., Hudson, OH.

SOCIAL

B 1-10	**I** 11-20	**N** 21-30	**G** 31-40	**O** 41-50
Say something positive about yourself.	Give a compliment to the person on your left.	Share something you would like to do but haven't.	Share a happy event in your life.	If you were given $10,000, what would you do with it?
Stand up and let everyone give you applause.	If you could change places with one person for a day, who would it be and why?	If you could meet one famous person in history, who would it be and why?	Share what you consider to be a personal accomplishment.	Give someone in the group a hug.
Talk about someone special in your life.	I feel best when people ___ ___ ___.	FREE	Describe your most prized possession.	Share what the greatest compliment is that you've received.
Give a compliment to the 2nd person on your left.	Describe something someone could do to help you feel happy.	Say something positive about yourself.	I am best at ___ ___ ___.	What is your favorite childhood memory?
What positive advice would you like to give to the President?	Describe what you consider a "perfect vacation".	Are you more like a gentle rain or a thunder-storm? Why?	Share what makes you a unique and special person.	Talk about 3 things you are grateful for.

SOCIAL BINGO

I. PURPOSE:

To increase social skills by playing a fun, easy and familiar game.

II. GENERAL COMMENTS:

Simple and familiar games can be used with individuals who are not acquainted, or with individuals who know each other very well. Sharing in a group setting is often easier in a structured manner, and games provide for a fun atmosphere. Questioning, listening and sharing are all important social skills experienced in this game.

III. POSSIBLE ACTIVITIES:

A. 1. Distribute one handout and 25 markers (paper clips, pennies, torn paper, etc.) per group member.

2. Instruct the individuals to write a number between 1 and 10 in each empty box below the "B" column, 11 and 20 in the "I" column, and so on.

3. Call random number/letter combinations, e.g., B-4, G-37, etc.

4. When a player has a square, he/she needs to do what that space asks.

5. When a player has a BINGO, he/she "wins" that round and can be given some token of achievement.

6. Play several times using typical BINGO variations: the "T" game, 4 corners, postage stamp, etc.

7. Process benefits of this activity.

B. 1. Cut Social Bingo sheet into 24 squares (deleting the FREE square) to make a social card game. Shuffle.

2. Distribute an even number of cards to each member.

3. Taking turns, instruct group members to turn to the person on their left and ask one of the questions on their cards.

4. Continue until all cards have been addressed, emphasizing appropriate question-asking, listening, and sharing throughout.

5. Process benefits of this structured social activity.

Activity handout submitted and facilitator's information adapted from submission by Lori Janssen, MSW, LGSW, CADC III, Fairmont, WV.

Causes of STRESS

Sometimes causes of stress are hidden. Take this opportunity to seek and find!

WORD SEEK

```
G C T F U C F Y R R O W K T H L A V
N G E C T J Q D N U C Q H Q Y Q G L
X A N X I N O L D I C R M G K M U Q
R M S I N L E I X I E H K D R J K R
X R U O T X F M L A V O I R E I B T
F H I E R S W N T L J O C L O A E A
R S L J S I U S O N N R R P D W T F
E L S S O L Y R M C I E G C L R F H
B Q L I W C T L T M R O S Z E H E S
T L F D Y D G V R S P I P S P G A N
Z B A A R R J E E E I G Z P S J N M
E T E Z M S N X S D G M F E A J I E
L G V W D I U M I Q B N C B P S D X
N J N Q H A L E N C A N A N X G I K
G X R A L W Y Y Y B A N V U L E S D
W G X I H E N K U N N P Z E X R J L
F O T P H C B S I W B U D I B B U G
U Y Q F T J E F B P R K S T H M T U
```

The following words are hidden in the puzzle:

ABUSE	DEATH	FINANCES	NOISE
ANGER	DISAPPOINTMENT	GRIEF	SEXUALITY
CHANGE	DIVORCE	ILLNESS	THREATS
CHILDREN	FAMILY	LOSS	WORK
CONFLICT	FEAR	MISTRUSTING	WORRY

Causes of *STRESS* Word-Seek

I. PURPOSE:

To increase knowledge and awareness of common causes of stress.

II. GENERAL COMMENTS:

People are often unaware of the causes of their stress. An activity that is enjoyable and cognitively challenging, can assist a person in identifying their life stressors.

III. POSSIBLE ACTIVITIES:

A. 1. Facilitate introductory discussion of stress.

2. Encourage group members to share own experiences with stress.

3. Instruct group members to individually complete word-seek after providing them with appropriate instructions.

4. Reconvene as a large group and discuss specific causes of stress as identified in word-seek.

5. Process benefits of greater self-awareness in regards to causes of stress.

B. 1. Initiate discussion of how causes of stress are often hidden, and that it is easy to be unaware of them.

2. Instruct group members on how to complete word-seek.

3. Distribute handouts and give group members 20-30 minutes to complete.

4. Share correct answers.

5. Discuss which of the causes of stress are presently being experienced by group members.

6. Ask group members to explore potential coping skills for each.

7. Process by asking group members what was learned from discussing causes of stress and potential coping skills.

Activity handout submitted by and facilitator's information adapted from submission by John R. Way, OTR/L, Corbin, KY.

A REAL MAN

Society often places stereotypical demands on people. There are many beliefs/expectations about what a man should be, should have, or should do. Complete each of the following sentences with as many responses as you think or feel belong.

A man is supposed to be _____

_____

_____.

A man is supposed to do _____

_____

_____.

A man is supposed to have _____

_____

_____.

A man is not supposed to be _____

_____

_____.

A man is not supposed to do _____

_____

_____.

A man is not supposed to have _____

_____

_____.

SEPARATING YOUR OWN BELIEFS / EXPECTATIONS FROM THOSE OF SOCIETY IS VERY CHALLENGING, YET CAN BE DONE!

Identify below, on the left, 3 beliefs/expectations from society that you would like to address in your own life, and on the right, the 3 revised beliefs/expectations you plan to adopt.

SOCIETY BELIEF / EXPECTATION	REVISED BELIEF / EXPECTATION
1.	
2.	
3.	

I. PURPOSE:

To help men (or women) identify the expectations and/or limitations put upon men in our culture today.

To help men (and women) be aware of the stress men experience from trying to live within these stereotypes.

II. GENERAL COMMENTS:

Biases and stereotypes restrict choices and decisions in life and can directly affect relationships. Becoming aware of expectations and limitations that men have accepted as "the way things are", without question, may help to free themselves. Being aware that others also experience some distress from these limits and expectations, will help men to accept themselves. This activity can be easily adapted to take a look at society's beliefs or expectations concerning women as well.

III. POSSIBLE ACTIVITIES:

A. 1. Distribute handouts, encouraging members of the group to complete with words, phrases, or sentences. You may wish to ask participants to distinguish their answers on a feeling level versus a thought-out, *politically correct* answer.

    2. Facilitate a discussion of each statement and what the impact is of feeling that one does not "measure up" to these identified beliefs/expectations and/or limitations.

    3. Process benefits of the activity and sharing.

B. 1. Put large sheets of newsprint on the walls around the room with each of the 6 phrases printed individually on a sheet. Ask group members to move about the room and write on the sheets with markers large enough to be read for the group as a whole later.

    2. Structure it differently in these ways:

       a. If all male (or all female) group, have participants write answers to questions in one color as they perceive "society's messages", and in another color their own personal beliefs if they are different.

       b. If a mixed gender group, have males write responses in one color and females in another.

    3. After either of the above activities, on new sheets of newsprint, write beliefs/expectations and limitations which are representative of the responses in one column, and in another column the challenges, problems, and/or distress experienced past and present related to each belief/expectation or limitation.

    4. Share benefits of the activity.

Activity handout and facilitator's information adapted from submission by Sue Bell-Milby, RNC, Wichita, KS.

$aving for $tress

Lifestyle habits play an important role in how well we cope with stress. Please complete the following questionnaire. After answering questions #1-20, total your "yes" and "no" answers. You receive 25 "Wellness Bucks" for each "yes", but must pay $25 for each "no". The total amount of "Wellness Bucks" you have, or don't have, may be symbolic of your ability to cope with the stress of day-to-day life situations.

	YES	NO
1. *I keep my mind young by continually learning.*	☐	☐
2. *I eat fresh fruits/vegetables each day.*	☐	☐
3. *I get seven to eight hours of sleep at least 4 nights per week.*	☐	☐
4. *I give and receive affection regularly.*	☐	☐
5. *I exercise to the point of perspiration at least twice a week.*	☐	☐
6. *I do not smoke/chew tobacco.*	☐	☐
7. *I take fewer than 5 alcoholic drinks a week.*	☐	☐
8. *I am the appropriate weight for my height.*	☐	☐
9. *I drink fewer than three cups of coffee (or other caffeine-rich drinks) a day.*	☐	☐
10. *I get strength from my religious/spiritual beliefs.*	☐	☐
11. *I attend clubs or social activities or do something fun at least once a week.*	☐	☐
12. *I have a network of friends and acquaintances.*	☐	☐
13. *I have one or more friends to confide in about personal matters.*	☐	☐
14. *I am in good health (including eyesight, hearing, and teeth).*	☐	☐
15. *I am usually able to speak openly about my feelings when angry or worried.*	☐	☐
16. *I spend some time on most days with work activities (household, children, employment, volunteering, etc.).*	☐	☐
17. *I am able to organize my time effectively.*	☐	☐
18. *I am able to budget my finances effectively.*	☐	☐
19. *I take some quiet time for myself during the day.*	☐	☐
20. *I can name three things I like about myself.*	☐	☐

Each Column total: ☐ ☐

x $25   x $25

receive: $ ☐   **owe:** $ ☐

I. PURPOSE:

To increase awareness of the "value" of a healthy lifestyle in managing stress and improving a sense of well-being.

II. GENERAL COMMENTS:

By placing monetary value on lifestyle habits, group members can see how choices they make can "cost" them well-being and stamina to face life's challenges. The more money (energy) spent on bad/unhealthy habits, the less money (energy) available for coping strategies. The focus is on how distress (stress gone bad) can be prevented.

III. POSSIBLE ACTIVITIES:

A. 1. Explain concept of "Saving for Stress". This shows how <u>valuable</u> healthy habits are in dealing with day-to-day situations.

   2. Assign one person to be the banker. Give banker several sheets of Wellness Bucks (form is in SUPPLEMENTAL SECTION of this book), photocopied on green paper.

   3. Distribute handouts and encourage members to complete as indicated on front of handout.

   4. Discuss as a group.

   5. Process benefits of a healthy lifestyle in managing stress.

B. 1. Follow steps in activity A.

   2. Encourage each member to name a stressful situation, e.g.,

      a. overslept

      b. the car won't start

      c. a child is ill

      d. it rains the day of the picnic

      e. an unexpected bill arrives

   3. All members pay facilitator $25 for each situation mentioned until several have no more money.

   4. Discuss the options for dealing with these stressful events. Review ways to build a "stress account" by reviewing questionnaire.

Activity handout and facilitator's information submitted by Patricia J. Eckwahl, RN, Jamestown, NY.

Congratulations
To

for

Congratulations To

PURPOSE:

To provide tangible recognition of accomplishments. These sheets may be used when a goal is met, at the time of discharge, or in celebration of an event. They can be placed on bulletin boards, in individual's rooms, in meeting rooms, and / or used as congratulatory cards.

DOCTOR LIST

Doctor's Name	Phone Number	Type of Doctor / Specialty
Dr.	—	
Dr.	—	
Dr.	—	
Dr.	—	
Dr.	—	
Dr.	—	
Dr.	—	
Dr.	—	

Police # _____   Emergency # _____

Fire # _____   Pharmacy # _____

Special Notes: _____

_____

_____

_____

Doctor List

PURPOSE:

To provide a quick reference of doctors, phone numbers, and areas of specialty, as well as other emergency telephone numbers (helpful as "refrigerator chart").

Happy
Birthday
to

_____

on your

Birthday!

Happy Birthday

PURPOSE:

To provide birthday well-wishes which can be signed by friends, acquaintances, staff, family, etc.

Home Program

Date: _____

Frequency: _____ x/day for _____

_____ x/week for _____

Precautions: _____

_____

Instructions:

Therapist: _____

If you have any questions, please

call us at _____ - _____.

Home Program

PURPOSE:

To provide specific information for use at home in order to maintain continuity of care.

Life Management Skills
ACTIVITY CHECKLIST ☑

ACTIVITY	DOING OK	NEED TO WORK ON	PLAN

LIFE MANAGEMENT SKILLS ACTIVITY CHECKLIST

PURPOSE:

To provide an organizational tool that will assist in evaluating strengths and deficits in various life management skills activities, as well as assist in developing action plans.

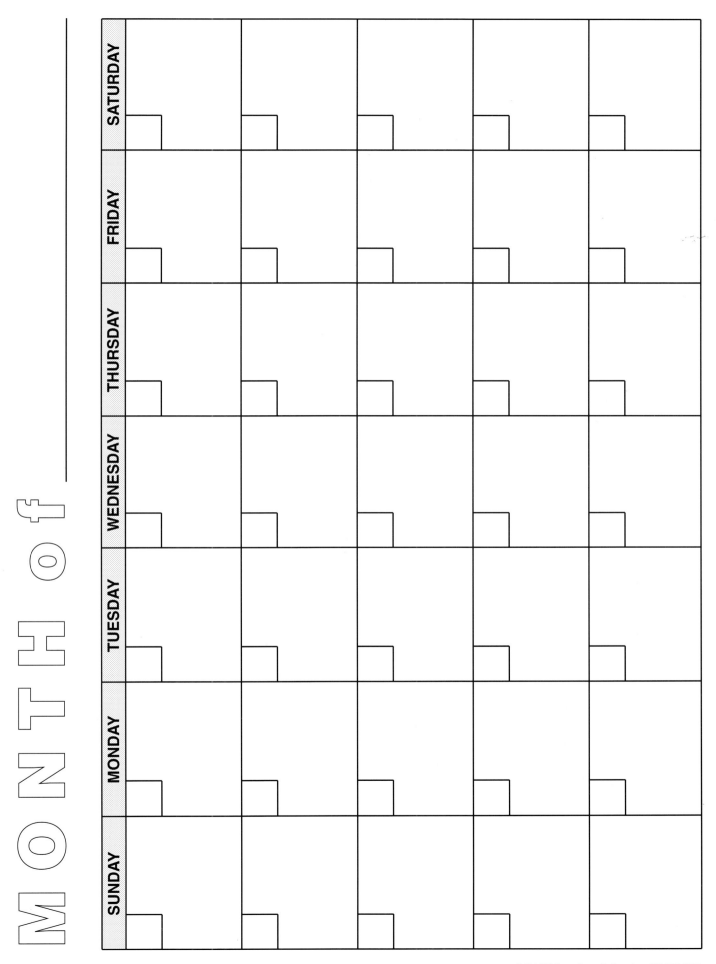

MONTH of _____

SUNDAY	MONDAY	TUESDAY	WEDNESDAY	THURSDAY	FRIDAY	SATURDAY

PURPOSE:

To provide a structured format for monthly appointments, responsibilities, holidays, celebrations and /or other individual or unit activities.

MY NAME IS

_____

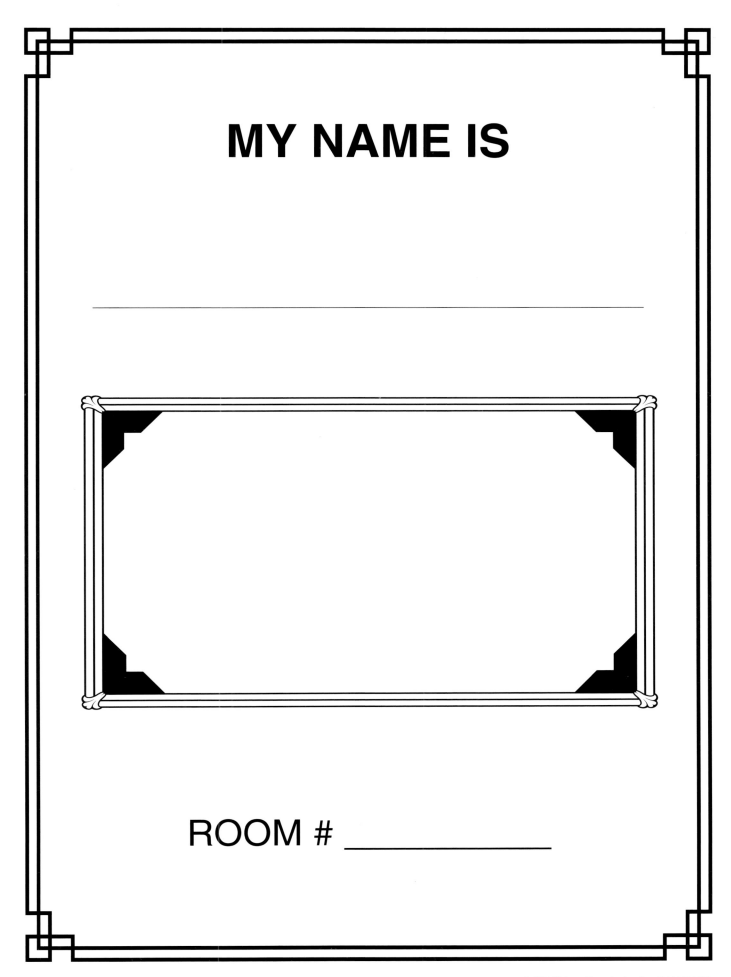

ROOM # _____

MY NAME IS

PURPOSE:

To provide creative visual cues to individuals who are disoriented. These visual cues might include names, room numbers, significant photographs, magazine cut-outs, swatches of material, drawings, etc., to help identify an individual's room.

MY TREATMENT PLAN

AREA NEEDING IMPROVEMENT	GOAL		TARGET DATE
①	G⊙AL 🎯		
②	G⊙AL 🎯		
③	G⊙AL 🎯		

My Signature _____

My Therapist's Signature _____

MY TREATMENT PLAN

PURPOSE:

To provide an individualized treatment plan encouraging personal responsibility for goal attainment.

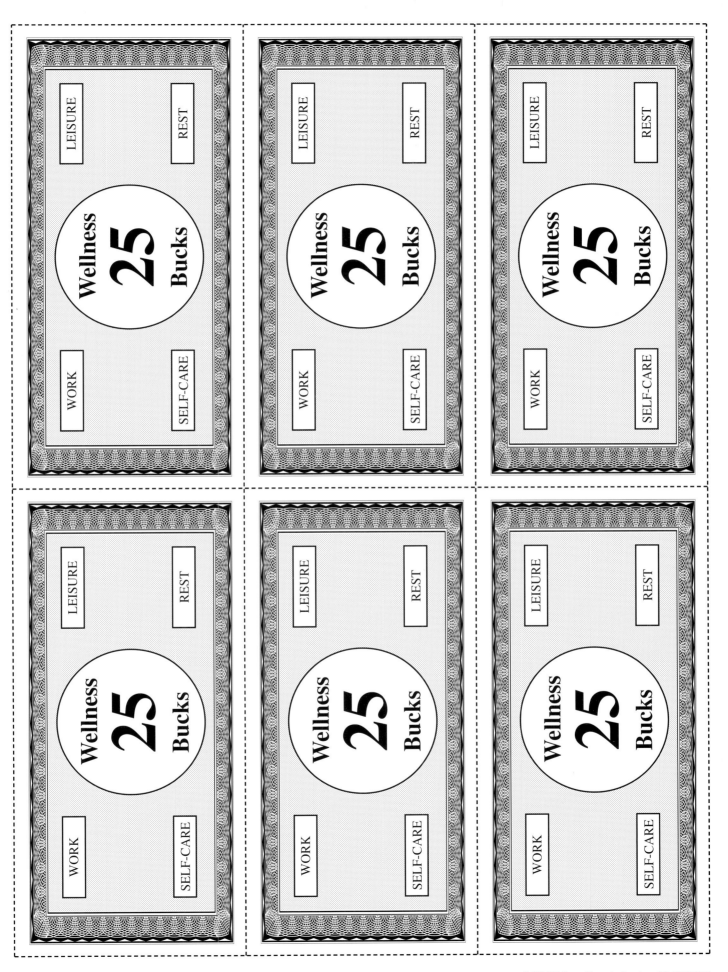

Wellness Bucks

PURPOSE:

To provide a token or reward for any wellness activity success. Can be creatively redeemed for gifts, coupons, samples, or other special privileges. <u>See Saving for Stress</u>, page 50, activities A and B, for a specific activity.

These are the Topics in the Life Management Skills Book Series.

Life Management Skills I, II, III, IV, V & VI Topics	LMS I	LMS II	LMS III	LMS IV	LMS V	LMS VI	Total Handouts
• Abuse					3		3
• Activities of Daily Living		2		2			4
• Aging			2		2		4
• Anger Management		6					6
• Anxiety/Fear						3	3
• Assertion	4	3					7
• Body Image			2				2
• Combating Stigma				2			2
• Communication		4	3	2			9
• Conflict Resolution			2				2
• Coping Skills			4	4	8		16
• Coping w/Serious Mental Illness				3			3
• Creative Expression			2			5	7
• Discharge Planning	2						2
• Emotion Identification	2						2
• Exercise	3						3
• Feedback			2				2
• Goal Setting	4					2	6
• Grief/Loss		3			3		6
• Healthy Living			3			4	7
• Home Management				4			4
• Humor		2		2			4
• Independent Living Skills						3	3
• Interpersonal Skills					2	3	5
• Job Readiness			2	2			4
• Journalizing				3			3
• Leisure	2			4	4	2	12
• Life Balance		3					3
• Making Changes					4		4
• Medication Management					4		4
• Money Management		3					3
• Motivation	2						2
• Nurturance			4				4
• Nutrition	3						3
• Parenting		2		3	2		7
• Personal Responsibility						2	2
• Positive Attitude					2	3	5
• Problem Solving	3						3
• Recovery/Relapse Prevention		3	2		4	8	17
• Relationships			5	4	4	3	16
• Reminiscence		3					3
• Responsibility				3			3
• Risk Taking	3						3
• Role Satisfaction	2		4				6
• Safety Issues		2					2
• Self-Awareness	3		4				7
• Self-Empowerment			2				2
• Self-Esteem	4	3	2	2	4	2	17
• Self-Expression					2		2
• Sexual Health				2			2
• Sleep	2						2
• Social Skills			2	2			4
• Spirituality						3	3
• Stress Management	3	2	3	6		5	19
• Suicide Issues				2			2
• Supports	2	2			2		6
• Time Management	3	3					6
• Therapeutic Treatment						2	2
• Values Clarification	3			2			5
TOTAL ACTIVITY HANDOUTS	50	50	50	50	50	50	300

(over)

Use these card games to facilitate development of Life Management Skills! Each deck of cards covers the wide variety of topics in its corresponding book. Since there are more cards than required for a typical 50-minute group session, you can choose the specific topics and cards that would be most beneficial for your intended population and setting.

You can liven up groups with relevant topic cards. Teach by 'DOING'! Use these open-ended cards, integrating knowledge while playing a card game! Each deck of cards corresponds with one of the Life Management Skills books. In the lower right corner of each card is the page number of its corresponding book. Can be used alone or with corresponding books.

---

18 FOCUS TOPICS including: Discharge Planning, Emotion Identification, Goal Setting, Motivation, Nutrition, Problem Solving, Risk-Taking, Role-Satisfaction and more.

Here are some examples from 4 of the other topics:

VALUES CLARIFICATION: *What qualities do you value in the people you deal with regularly (honesty, loyalty, trust, sincerity, intelligence, etc.)?*

STRESS MANAGEMENT: *How do you presently cope with a difficult situation in your life? How can you improve your coping skills?*

SELF-AWARENESS: *When was the last time you truly felt good about yourself? What were the circumstances?*

ASSERTION: *Describe one way you can better communicate with someone important in your life.*

63 cards + 9 blanks to fill in your own!
(Corresponds with Life Management Skills I)

| PRDW-71011 Self-Manager I cards | $15.95 |

---

18 FOCUS TOPICS including: Communication, Grief and Loss, Life-Balance, Money Management, Parenting, Reminiscence, Steps to Recovery and more.

Here are some examples from 4 of the other topics:

TIME MANAGEMENT: *Can you be counted on to be on time? Why or why not?*

SUPPORT SYSTEMS: *Is it easy for you to accept help? Will you ask for help when you need it?*

ANGER MANAGEMENT: *What is something that sparks your anger? How do you handle it?*

SELF-ESTEEM: *When you are given a compliment, do you usually acknowledge or accept it? Do you suggest that you really don't deserve it?*

63 cards + 9 blanks to fill in your own!
(Corresponds with Life Management Skills II)

| PRDW-71012 Self-Manager II cards | $15.95 |

---

18 FOCUS TOPICS including: Aging, Body Image, Conflict Resolution, Creative Expression, Feedback, Healthy Living, Nurturance, Self-Empowerment and more.

Here are some examples from 4 of the other topics:

COPING SKILLS: *Have you ever used "writing" . . . writing letters, journal writing, or poetry - as a way to learn more about yourself or to cope with stress? If yes, describe. If no, would you try?*

RELATIONSHIPS: *Do you feel fatigued after spending time with a certain friend or relative? Who and why?*

JOB READINESS: *What are 3 benefits of women working outside of the home?*

SOCIAL SKILLS: *What is a label, stereotype, or prejudice that offends you? Why?*

63 cards + 9 blanks to fill in your own!
(Corresponds with Life Management Skills III)

| PRDW-71013 Self-Manager III cards | $15.95 |

---

18 FOCUS TOPICS including: Activities of Daily Living, Serious Mental Illness, Relationships, Responsibility, Sexual Health, Suicide Prevention/Awareness, Values and more.

Here are some examples from 4 of the other topics:

COMMUNICATION: *Name 3 topics that you can talk about with someone you've just met. What are 3 things not to talk about with someone you hardly know?*

JOURNALIZING: *I have learned _____ about my mood/illness/health.*

HUMOR: *Name 3 things, or people, that always make you laugh.*

STRESS MANAGEMENT: *How long do you tend to hold on to anger or hurt feelings? How do you let go?*

63 cards + 9 blanks to fill in your own!
(Corresponds with Life Management Skills IV)

| PRDW-71014 Self-Manager IV cards | $15.95 |

---

15 FOCUS TOPICS including: Coping Skills, Grief, Interpersonal Skills, Leisure, Parenting, Positive Attitude, Self-Expression and more.

Here are some examples from 4 of the other topics:

MEDICATION MANAGEMENT: *What are "over-the-counter" medications for? Compare them with prescription medications.*

RECOVERY: *What are symptoms of your illness that warn you when it may reoccur?*

ABUSE: *If someone asks you to go out with them and your intuition tells you not to, what can you do and say?*

MAKING CHANGES: *What are 3 unhealthy eating habits you have?*

63 cards + 9 blanks to fill in your own!
(Corresponds with Life Management Skills V)

| PRDW-71015 Self-Manager V cards | $15.95 |

---

15 FOCUS TOPICS including: Goal Setting, Healthy Living, Personal Responsibility, Positive Outlook, Relationships, Self-Esteem, Spirituality and more.

Here are some examples from 4 of the other topics:

ANXIETY/FEAR: *Finish the sentence: I am fearful of _____. Explain.*

EXPRESSIVE THERAPY: *If you were a 'super-hero' – what would two of your 'super-skills' be?*

INDEPENDENT LIVING SKILLS: *What benefits are, or would, be important to you in a job?*

THERAPEUTIC TREATMENT: *What role does 'trust' play in your Doctor/Patient relationships? How about your personal relationships?*

63 cards + 9 blanks to fill in your own!
(Corresponds with Life Management Skills VI)

| PRDW-71016 Self-Manager VI cards | $15.95 |

WELLNESS REPRODUCTIONS & PUBLISHING, LLC
A Guidance Channel Company

Call for catalogue 800 / 669-9208
or Fax 800 / 501-8120
e-mail: info@wellness-resources.com
website: http://www.wellness-resources.com

Wellness Reproductions Makes It Easy To Order!
ORDER ONLINE 24-HOURS A DAY, CALL, FAX or MAIL US

① BILLING INFORMATION

First Name | Last Name | MI

Title or Initials | Department

Organization/Facility

Street Address | Suite or Apt. No.

City | State | Zip + four

Phone | Fax

E-mail Address

SHIPPING INFORMATION *(IF another address or your business address):*

First Name | Last Name | MI

Title or Initials | Department

Organization/Facility

Street Address | Suite or Apt. No.

City | State | Zip + four

Phone | Fax

E-mail Address

② ORDERING INFORMATION

Order Code	Name of Product/Description	Page No.	Quantity	Price Each	Total Price
PRDW71003	Life Management Skills III book	—		$ 44.95	
PRDW71013	Self-Manager III cards (corresponds with Life Management Skills III)	—		$ 15.95	
PRDW71000D	KIT – Life Management Skills III book and cards (save $5.95)	—		$ 54.95	
PRDW71000A	KIT – Life Management Skills I, II, III, IV, V, VI and VII (save $44.70)	—		$ 269.95	
PRDW71010	KIT – All 7 Self-Manager cards (save $11.70)	—		$ 99.95	
PRDW71000	KIT – All 7 Life Management Skills books and cards (save $56.35)	—		$ 369.95	
PRDW71219	HEALTHY RELATIONSHIPS laminated poster – 24" x 36"	31		$ 15.95	
PRDW71249	POSITIVE MENTAL ATTITUDE laminated poster – 24" x 36"	12		$ 15.95	
PRDW71252	RESOLVING CONFLICTS laminated poster – 24" x 36"	8		$ 15.95	
PRDW71277	ROAD TO RECOVERY laminated poster – 24" x 36"	28		$ 15.95	

③ PAYMENT METHOD

☐ Check or money order in U.S. funds.
☐ Purchase Order (must be attached) P.O. # _____

☐ Visa   ☐ MasterCard   ☐ American Express

Account Number   Expiration Date

Print Name _____   Signature (required) _____

Subtotal	
*Shipping & Handling	
Subtotal	
NY and OH Sales Tax	
GRAND TOTAL	

100% **GUARANTEE:** *Wellness Reproductions & Publishing, LLC* stands behind its products 100%. We will refund, exchange or credit your account for the price of any materials returned **within 30 days** of receipt (excluding shipping). ALL MERCHANDISE NEEDS TO BE IN PERFECT, RESALE-ABLE CONDITION. Simply call us at 1-800-669-9208 for a return authorization number.

IMPORTANT INFORMATION: Our Order Policies ensure fast, efficient service!

Ordering Made Easy!
Have your order code ready!

Online
www.wellness-resources.com
(with credit card – **secured!**)

Call **1.800.669.9208**

Fax **1.800.501.8120**
Toll-Free 24-hours / 7 days

Mail
**Wellness Reproductions
& Publishing, LLC**
135 Dupont St.• P.O. Box 760
Plainview, NY 11803-0760

SHIPPING & HANDLING:
REGULAR GROUND: Add *10% (minimum $5.95)* in 48 contiguous states.
For Alaska, Hawaii, Puerto Rico, Canada and all other international locations; and for rush, express or overnight delivery, please call for rates and delivery information.
Shipments outside of the United States may be subject to additional handling charges and fees. Customers are responsible for any applicable taxes and duties.

PAYMENT METHOD:
CHECK: Make your check payable to *Wellness Reproductions & Publishing, LLC.*
OPEN ACCOUNT: We accept purchase orders from recognized public or private institutions. New accounts please call for information on how to set up an account.
P.O. TERMS: Purchase orders, net 30 days.

CREDIT CARDS: Please include account number, expiration date and your signature.
F.O.B. NY. All international orders must be prepaid in U.S. Funds.

OTHER:
SALES TAX: New York and Ohio residents, add sales tax on total, including shipping and handling. Tax-exempt organizations, please provide exempt or resale number when ordering.

DELIVERY: We ship all in-stock items within the contiguous 48 states via UPS or USPS. Back orders are items that are currently out of stock, but will be shipped to you as soon as possible. There is no additional cost for shipping and handling of back orders if shipped separately from your original order. Please allow up to 7-10 working days for delivery.

PRICING: This order form supersedes all previous order forms. Prices subject to change without notice. If this form has expired, we will bill you any difference in price.

UNIVERSITY INSTRUCTOR? If you are considering using this book as a school text or supplemental resource, please call our office to discuss desk copies and quantity education discounts.

UPDATE OUR MAILING LIST: You are automatically added to our mailing list when you order your first product from us. If you want to change your address, remove your name, or eliminate duplicate names from our file, please contact us. We sometimes make available our mailing list to outside parties. If you do not wish to have your information shared, please let us know.

Please photocopy, complete and mail to Wellness Reproductions and Publishing, LLC, P.O. Box 760 • Plainview, New York 11803-0760

FEEDBACK - LIFE MANAGEMENT SKILLS III

1. Check the topics that were of special interest to you in LMS III.

____ Aging	____ Feedback	____ Roles
____ Body Image	____ Healthy Living	____ Self-Awareness
____ Communication	____ Job Readiness	____ Self-Empowerment
____ Conflict Resolution	____ Nurturance	____ Self-Esteem
____ Coping Skills	____ Relapse Prevention	____ Social Skills
____ Creative Expression	____ Relationships	____ Stress Management

2. What topics would be of interest in future publications?

a) _____

b) _____

c) _____

3. Which were your favorite handouts?

a) _____

b) _____

c) _____

4. Describe an activity that you have created for any of the pages in this book.

_____

_____

_____

If this activity can be published in our WELLNESS net•work newsletter or website, please sign with your professional initials for publication. If it is selected, you will receive a $25 WELLNESS gift certificate.

(signature) _____

5. Comments on LMS III: _____

_____

_____

Can these comments be published?   _____ Yes   _____ No

(signature) _____   *(date)* _____

Name _____   Title _____

Facility _____   Occupation _____

Address _____   Home Address _____

City _____   City _____

State _____ Zip _____   State _____ Zip _____

Phone (work) (____) _____   Phone (home) (____) _____

email _____   Fax _____

(SEE REVERSE SIDE FOR ORDER FORM)